"In *The God Guarantee*, Jack Alexander exposes fear as the underlying enemy of generous living and giving. He calls us to trust God and value community, and he makes it easier to do so with the perspectives he brings and the stories he tells."

—**Randy Alcorn**, author of *The Treasure Principle*

"Jack Alexander is a close friend, mentor, brother, and successful businessman who is one of the most insightful students of Scripture I know. Some books reinforce what I already know and others say it better than I've heard it before, but great books create a 'paradigm shift' in my mind to see life, God, and myself like never before. *The God Guarantee* is one of those books and I highly recommend it."

—**Chip Ingram**, teaching pastor for Living on the Edge; author of *The Real God*

"Jack Alexander engages in deep, radical thinking about our lives in God's world. He sees that the gestures of Holy Communion (take, bless, break, give) readily morph into the truths of our daily lives. From there he ponders inviting holiness into our lives, whereby everything (including our money) is transformed. I find Jack's theological sensibility both acute and reliable, and I am grateful for his witness."

—**Walter Brueggemann**, professor emeritus at Columbia Theological Seminary; author of *The Prophetic Imagination*

"Jack drills deeply into the topic of fear and helps us identify where we are in our belief systems and how to move into the freedom of the abundant life Jesus promised. . . . I highly recommend this book, as I know it will be a guide and an encouragement."

—**Ron Blue**, founding director of Kingdom Advisors and Ronald Blue & Company; author of *Master Your Money*

"Far too often we base our security on our own efforts and stock-piled resources rather than on God's repeated guarantee to care for his children. Jack Alexander insightfully illustrates how true security comes from knowing and believing in the Lord who multiplied the loaves and fishes, giving us the confidence to reach out to others as he calls us to do."

—**Jim Daly**, president of Focus on the Family; author of *The Good Dad*

"*The God Guarantee* is a must-read for everyone who names Christ and will give you a truly accurate biblical understanding of prosperity and scarcity. . . . While this book does not claim to be theological, it is filled with solid biblical theology. It is a book you will read again and again."

—**Michael Youssef**, president of Leading the Way Ministries

"I am deeply grateful that my friend Jack Alexander has written this book. He reminds us that the generosity journey is a spiritual one. It begins with understanding God's perfect example of generosity and manifests in our move from duty to devotion. This makes this book less about giving and more about generous living."

—**Jay Hein**, president of the Sagamore Institute; former director of the White House Office of Faith-Based and Community Initiatives

"This book is both heartwarming and provocative. It will warm your heart by revealing the largeness of God in fresh, new ways. It provokes, not through guilt manipulation, but by fostering a desire to attain all God intended for us."

—**John D. Beckett**, chairman and CEO of the R.W. Beckett Corporation; author of *Loving Monday* and *Mastering Monday*

"Despite the certainty of our salvation in Christ, we struggle to believe that God intended us to live an abundant life. We alternate between the extremes of hope and despair, reluctant to rest in the guarantee of God's provision. Jack Alexander opens up his heart and life experience to help us discard scarcity thinking in favor of the God-given promise of abundance."

—**Cheryl A. Bachelder**, former CEO of Popeyes Louisiana Kitchen; author of *Dare to Serve*

"As a person who often battles anxiety concerning provision for the future, I've found in Jack's book a lifeline about the reality of God's abundant nature. My faith in God's commitment to me has been strengthened in knowing Jack and reading this book."

—**Todd Harper**, president of Generous Giving

"When Jack Alexander invited God into the world of his business dealings, he had no idea what treasures he would discover. His amazing business successes pale in comparison to the golden spiritual nuggets he has uncovered and chronicled in *The God Guarantee*."

—**Robert Lupton**, founder and president of FCS Urban Ministries; author of *Toxic Charity*

"In *The God Guarantee*, Jack Alexander answers the fundamental question, 'Will I have enough?' Jack helps us understand that because of our great God's love and care for us, not only will we have everything we need, but we are also free to be generous to others."

—**Dr. Crawford W. Loritts Jr.**, pastor, author, speaker, and radio host

"This book masterfully connects the dots between faith, community, generosity, and real life. Read it now and your view of possibility will be greater!"

—**Jeff Shinabarger**, founder of Plywood People; author of *More or Less*

"I love to give. I love being around givers; therefore, to read a book written by a giver genuinely ministers to me. *The God Guarantee* deals with the reality of fear. Learn how fear was never intended to paralyze you but to inspire you to be generous."

—**Johnny Hunt**, senior pastor, First Baptist Church Woodstock

"Modern society has perfected the art of telling us we are never enough. Meanwhile, God tells us we are enough because he is enough. And there's the tension. Who will we believe? Jack invites us to live in the freedom of enough and to experience the joy of a generous life."

—**Pamela Pugh**, cofounder and chairman of the board,
Women Doing Well Initiatives

"Physicians know not to treat symptoms, but to treat the problem causing the symptoms. Jack identifies the root problem for feeling there is not enough money, time to serve, or emotional energy to give of ourselves. He then skillfully uses many personal and biblical examples to create a solution to this core problem—by creating a feeling of security and capacity."

—**Richard L. Jackson**, CEO, Jackson Healthcare

"Fear is the primary adversary of a generous life. Jack clearly unpacks the certainty and pattern of God's provision—and helps us overcome this fear."

—**Daryl Heald**, founder of Generosity Path

THE GOD
GUARANTEE

THE GOD
GUARANTEE

*Finding Freedom from
the Fear of Not Having Enough*

JACK ALEXANDER

BakerBooks
a division of Baker Publishing Group
Grand Rapids, Michigan

Published by Baker Books
a division of Baker Publishing Group
P.O. Box 6287, Grand Rapids, MI 49516-6287
www.bakerbooks.com

Printed in the United States of America

Library of Congress Cataloging-in-Publication Data is on file at the Library of Congress, Washington, DC.

Paperback Edition ISBN 978-0-8010-7528-5
Special Edition ISBN 978-0-8010-7746-3

Unless otherwise indicated, Scripture quotations are from the Holy Bible, New International Version®. NIV®. Copyright © 1973, 1978, 1984, 2011 by Biblica, Inc.™ Used by permission of Zondervan. All rights reserved worldwide. www.zondervan.com

Scripture quotations labeled ESV are from The Holy Bible, English Standard Version® (ESV®), copyright © 2001 by Crossway, a publishing ministry of Good News Publishers. Used by permission. All rights reserved. ESV Text Edition: 2011

Scripture quotations labeled KJV are from the King James Version of the Bible.

Scripture quotations labeled NKJV are from the New King James Version®. Copyright © 1982 by Thomas Nelson, Inc. Used by permission. All rights reserved.

Scripture quotations labeled Phillips are from The New Testament in Modern English, revised edition—J. B. Phillips, translator. © J. B. Phillips 1958, 1960, 1972. Used by permission of Macmillan Publishing Co., Inc.

The author is represented by Alive Literary Agency, 7680 Goddard Street, Suite 200, Colorado Springs, CO 80920, www.aliveliterary .com.

17 18 19 20 21 22 23   7 6 5 4 3 2 1

In keeping with biblical principles of creation stewardship, Baker Publishing Group advocates the responsible use of our natural resources. As a member of the Green Press Initiative, our company uses recycled paper when possible. The text paper of this book is composed in part of post-consumer waste.

To Lisa . . .
my loving wife and a model of holistic generosity.

To Randy Pope . . .
my faithful pastor, mentor and friend.

Contents

Contents

Foreword

The book you are about to read by Jack Alexander doesn't fit neatly into any of the typical contemporary Christian book categories.

It's not a self-help book. In fact, it's sharply critical of the "you can have a great life today" literature. It actually tells us to *expect* that things will sometimes go wrong, that we will be broken, that things will fall apart. However, there is a deeply biblical, hopeful realism here—that troubles will come, yet our afflictions can turn us into something great (see 2 Corinthians 4:17). Jack shows us that only through the furnace of affliction can our ore become gold or our coal become diamonds.

It is also not a conventional book on stewardship, which would lay out all the reasons why and how and how much you should give. Those are important, but in this volume Jack goes deeper—and moves earlier in the sequence of motivation. He has wisely discerned that most people's resources are locked away, hardly to be shared, perhaps even despite sound biblical and practical arguments, because of a particular kind of heart attitude that makes generosity hard. What is it?

This book understands that at the root of an ungenerous heart is not mere stinginess or greed but *fearfulness*. Accruing resources is often a way we try to take control of our own world and fend for ourselves because we fear we can't trust God. That is the reason we don't see what Jack calls the capacity of so many situations for doing good. That is why we become crushed by suffering rather than growing through it. And that is why we are so ungenerous with ourselves and our assets. America is filled with comfortably prosperous people who mostly feel they don't have enough. They are dominated and controlled by a pervasive sense of resource scarcity and precariousness.

Jack confronts this problem directly to clear the way for a life of vision, durability, joy, and generosity. He does so through two crucial insights.

First, he shows that fear is fundamentally selfish. In our fear, we do not think of ourselves as being self-absorbed, but 1 John 4:18 tells us that the opposite of love is not hate but fear. This is so because love makes us think of others, while fear makes us think mainly of ourselves. Love always makes us vulnerable. Fear refuses that vulnerability and makes self-protection the priority. So to become more generous, we must first deal with the self-absorbed fear that keeps us from trusting God and loving others.

Second, Jack observes that our practice of biblical generosity is one key to our *own* provision. God demonstrates that he provides for us in and through our relationships—first with him, then with others.

Throughout the book, Jack uses Jesus's miracle of the loaves and fish to illustrate God's pattern for provision. Let me reinforce his main ideas by pointing to another Bible passage that speaks to this important issue of how Christians can move from a spirit of scarcity and fear to one of abundance and provision.

In Acts 4, we read of a community of deep economic sharing and generosity:

> All the believers were one in heart and mind. No one claimed that any of their possessions was their own, but they shared everything they had. With great power the apostles continued to testify to the resurrection. . . . From time to time those who owned lands or houses sold them, brought the money from the sales and put it at the apostles' feet, and it was distributed to anyone who had need. (vv. 32–35)

It was also a community where "they were all filled with the Holy Spirit and spoke the word of God boldly" (v. 31). We learn here that a basic mark of being Spirit-filled is boldness. Why is that? Romans 8:15–16 illustrates that the Spirit's work is to oppose a spirit of fear. If the Holy Spirit brings the opposite of fearfulness, the mark of Spirit-filledness would of course be fear*less*ness. But, specifically, how does the Holy Spirit make us fearless? The Romans passage tells us that the Spirit assures us that we are children of God. (In the same way, the Spirit assured and empowered Jesus for ministry at his baptism, saying, "This is my Son, whom I love; with him I am well pleased" [Matthew 17:5].)

This, then, is the nature of Spirit-boldness: it is a deep assurance of the Father's love for us personally through Christ.

The Acts text shows us that this assurance of God's love influences not only our words but also our actions. Luke clearly saw the lifestyle of radical giving of ourselves and the sharing of our resources as proceeding from a heart that has been changed through the filling of the Holy Spirit.

What if this sense of assurance is missing? Look at financial generosity. Most people do not come close to meeting the biblical guideline on giving (10 percent of our income or a "tithe"; see Malachi 3:8–10; Luke 11:42). Why? Giving means we have less stored away in case of a crisis—it's a security issue. Giving means the people we give to might misuse the money—it's a control issue. Giving means we can't think of ourselves as securely wealthy—it's a self-esteem issue. At the root of all these issues is fear and lack of trust.

But the reality of God's saving love, brought home in assurance by the Holy Spirit, changes that fear. We see that God is far more committed to our good than we believed. Look at what he did through Jesus! We see, then, that God can be trusted. Jesus is now more "precious" (1 Peter 2:7) than anything else. When we have him, even diamonds look expendable.

This is not a self-help book, though Jack reminds us that we do have a responsibility and a role to play in overcoming scarcity. God uses our generosity in relationships to provide for others—and to provide for us.

This is not a stewardship book, though I would consider it an excellent "pre-stewardship" resource. Jack knows that the question "Will I have enough?" always comes before "Why, what, and how am I to give?" Possibly the greatest service this book renders to the church is to answer that first question convincingly so that the next ones can be answered with freedom and joy.

One more observation about Jack's insightful, helpful volume. It's not a devotional. But it will send you to your knees.

Dr. Timothy Keller
Chairman, Redeemer City to City

Acknowledgments

Every book is a journey. I want to thank Larry Powell, Mark MacDonald, Todd Harper, Howard Dayton, and Chuck Bentley on their initial encouragements and insights to begin the journey. Our generosity work at the Reimagine Group, among hundreds of churches, provided substantial insights and data that holistic generosity is, in fact, the better way. My wife, Lisa, has been a wonderful model of holistic generosity and profound thoughtfulness in the lives of others.

None of our work would have gotten off the ground without the support and encouragement from Raymond Harris, Tom Darden, Jim and Jan Bisenius, Mike Last, Daryl Heald, Chris Maclellan, and Tom Lowe.

Lisa Jackson, Rick Christian, and the team at Alive Literary were not only invaluable but also had the courage to totally redirect our direction toward the "elephant in the room"—the fear that most of us experience as we grapple with the very real scarcity we can experience in our world. They encouraged me to press into reconciling God's promises and provisions in overcoming this fear and having people lean into faith and holistic generosity.

Thanks go to Beth Jusino who helped mightily with assisting me in writing and completing this book. Our production team members, including Matt Pope, Tim Dalrymple, and Drew Kimball all provided thousands of hours of work and insights. Special thanks go to Patty Wyngaard who spent so many hours working through the refinement of the book's message as well as coordinating work on the manuscript with Beth, Baker, and others.

I also want to thank my sister, Beth Baumert, who graciously took the time to review and proof the manuscript.

Finally, the whole team at Baker enthusiastically got behind this project. Special thanks go to Chad Allen, Amy Ballor, Eileen Hanson, Mark Rice, Erin Smith, and Brianna DeWitt. They had a belief and passion that this message could provide healing and new outcomes to many.

Thanks also to Tim Keller who wrote the foreword and focused all readers on the importance of finding freedom from this fear of scarcity and recognizing that fear, not hate, is the opposite of love.

I am grateful to the Lord for his patience, grace, and help in my time of need as I have overcome many of my own fears.

Introduction

Searching for Enough

By anyone's standards, Jaden Hayes has had a hard childhood. His father died when he was four, and then just two years later, Jaden discovered his mother's body after she died in her sleep.

The six-year-old boy stoically endured another funeral and then went to live with his aunt. According to multiple news reports, he told her he was "tired of all the sad faces." He wanted to know how to make people happy again. She suggested the best way to make someone smile is to smile at them first. And so, just weeks after his mother's death, Jaden began what's become known as the Smile Experiment. He and his aunt went into the city of Savannah, near their Georgia home, and approached people who looked sad or serious. Jaden would smile at them and—to hedge his bets— offer them a small toy.

"It's like sheer joy came out of this child," said his aunt. "And the more people that he made smile, the more this light shone."[1]

I first heard about Jaden and his experiment more than a year ago, and it still brings tears to my eyes every time I think about it. I wasn't the only one who was touched. National media picked up Jaden's story, and people across the country responded with gifts, including photos of their own smiles for Jaden.

What made Jaden's story so special that it became a national movement? It spoke to the feelings of loss and hopelessness that are all too familiar to many of us today. We look at Jaden and wonder, *How could a boy who lost so much be able to give so much?*

Instead of giving in, as we are so often tempted to do, Jaden Hayes overcame. In a world driven by isolation, doubt, and, perhaps most of all, scarcity, this boy found a way through.

Not Enough

Scarcity is a word that has come up often in the past decade. Everyone from psychologists to advertising executives to talk-show guests have tried to explain, and sometimes capitalize on, the ways scarcity shapes us as humans. But when we take away all the scientific talk, what does it really mean?

The sense of scarcity, simply defined, is the fear that there is too little of something to go around—that there might be too little for us.

What if I don't have enough to retire?

How will I pay these medical bills?

Can we really afford to have a child?

But the insidious effects of a scarcity mentality go even deeper. The fear of "not enough" affects our spirits as well as our wallets.

Do I have enough time to invest in this new project?

Do I have the emotional energy to get involved with that person in need?

What if I don't have enough left for me?

These questions, and many like them, plague our culture. Ever since the Great Recession, many of the people I meet struggle with a sense of loss and a dark view of the future. I've talked with dozens of families who feel as if they live on the edge of a knife, worrying that one unexpected bill or crisis will push them into a situation they can't afford. And when I look at the numbers, it's easy to see why.

Technology creates an "always-on" expectation, expanding the average length of the American workweek even as our paychecks decrease. The average American has not experienced an increase in his or her real income, adjusted for inflation, since 2000. Our retirement accounts have shriveled up, and working adults who once felt stable now take on crushing debt to cover the skyrocketing costs of education and health care. Class warfare dominates the landscape as the gap between the rich and the poor reaches record levels. For the first time in American history, the next generation of working- and middle-class adults is not likely to surpass their parents' generation in education, income, or opportunity.

However, the problems that plague us are about far more than the size of our bank accounts. Our stress levels are rising, and our spirits are stretched as thin as our budgets. A steady stream of tragedy and scandal fills the news, leaving us feeling helpless as we double lock our doors and eye every stranger with suspicion. The culture demands that we not offend anyone, even as the tone of public debates and discourse grows uglier by the day.

In short, the messages all around us tell us to be afraid—and it's easy to believe them.

Fear is a suffocating emotion. It leaves us feeling selfish, bitter, and disconnected from others. Scarcity is an offshoot of fear that makes us see the world as zero sum, where anything you get means there's less for me. If I give some of myself or my resources, then there won't be enough left for my needs.

There's just not enough—whether we're talking about money, trust, or even love—to go around. Bit by bit, the resulting sense of scarcity grinds us down into hopelessness.

At least that was my experience. It's important for you to know this isn't just a book about other people's problems. For much of my life, fear and scarcity were my own constant companions.

I met them when my father, like Jaden's, died unexpectedly. I was only nine years old. My mother remarried, but it was not a happy union. In fact, my mother and her husband seemed to hate each other for most of their marriage. Growing up, I heard endless fights about money. They argued about small things, like what account to use to pay certain bills or what to do with small and sentimental inheritances. According to my stepfather, there was never enough.

He was just as stingy emotionally as he was with the single dollar he put into the church offering plate each week. My sisters and I were not encouraged to dream. Instead, we were scolded if we did not achieve. There was no grace, no safety net.

I responded by working harder. If no one else could be trusted to meet my needs, I reasoned, I would have to do it myself. I delivered newspapers during never-ending, icy New England winters and caddied at the country clubs during the long, humid summers. I worked long hours as a busboy and rode the late-night bus home.

My world was a world of scarcity. We had no excess money or love or comfort. I learned not to expect them. Instead, I worked throughout college and studied business and accounting—the safe, smart, responsible choice. After college, I took a job in accounting. I supported myself comfortably, and, on the outside, everything was fine.

Yet everything was not fine. The lessons we learn as children stick with us, and my childhood teacher was fear. It kept me from taking risks, from following my heart. It made me see everything in life as a competition. I started gambling my income in poker games. If I didn't win, I felt as if I would die.

My life was missing something, and I felt as if I was always struggling to avoid falling into a hole.

When I was twenty-five, I wrote the "10 Rules of Alexander," an idealistic and self-motivating challenge designed to get me out of a rut. One of the rules was this: if I ever had $10,000—almost a year's salary at the time—I would quit my job and do whatever I wanted to do.

This was the only way I could see to get past the fear. I couldn't imagine how I would get that kind of money, but if some miracle happened, I was sure the security that would come with so much wealth would solve my most pressing and deepest concerns.

It didn't, of course. Over the following years, my career grew, and I saw $10,000 and more pass through my bank account. More importantly, I became a Christian, and my spiritual life blossomed. I married a wonderful woman, and we raised three sons. I lived a life of outward success and fulfillment. But even then the fear never really went away.

Scarcity moved into my life when I was nine years old, and it didn't move out until much later, through a series of events I'll tell you about in part 4 of this book.

All the money in the world can't cover a deeply embedded sense of scarcity. In fact, researcher and bestselling author Brené Brown says, "Worrying about scarcity is our culture's version of post-traumatic stress. It happens when we've been through too much, and rather than coming together to heal (which requires vulnerability) we're angry and scared and at each other's throats."[2]

This isn't a problem affecting only the middle class either. The feeling of scarcity impacts every level of society. In a 2015 survey of American millionaires, more than half said they did not feel financially secure. Most reported they worried an unexpected change—a job loss, a market crash, or a failed investment—could affect their lifestyle at any moment. Fifty-two percent said they felt "stuck on a treadmill." At every level of wealth evaluated in the survey, respondents said they need double what they have in order to feel secure.[3]

Yet a young boy named Jaden, who had almost nothing, found a way through this sense of scarcity. What did a six-year-old boy know that the richest people in the country don't?

Caught between Two Lies

According to theologian Walter Brueggemann, scarcity first emerged in ancient Egypt, in the time of Pharaoh. According to Genesis 41, Pharaoh dreamt there would be a famine in his land, and that made him afraid. His fear encouraged the first recorded application of scarcity into an economy.

Pharaoh began to hoard grain and resources, taking control of what was not originally his.[4]

Fast-forward almost thirty-five hundred years, and government and secular entities are still the primary conduits of scarcity messages. Taxes take what we have. Media fills us with a lust for bigger houses, better clothes, and more possessions. The modern education system tells us our bodies are random mutations of cells, accidents of evolution that live in an arbitrary system that rewards "the survival of the fittest" and eliminates everything else.

During the best periods of human history, the Christian church countered those messages by pointing to a bigger, divinely inspired picture, balancing the narrative. A weekly Sabbath pulled us away from the race for money and reminded us to focus on a loving, powerful, and eternal God. The Scriptures reminded us that there is a higher purpose, and eternal life, waiting for us.

But as the split between the church and the culture grew, the balance slipped. And Christians today are not exempt from a scarcity mentality. They too worry about rising costs and stagnant incomes. Their time also is stretched to the breaking point in the digital age, and they are just as saturated as non-Christians with images and stories highlighting the hurt, brokenness, and lack in the world.

They also have questions.

Can God really meet our needs?

How can we say God loves us if it seems as if he's not adequately providing for us?

Sure, once upon a time God may have given his people manna to eat. But where is he today? What is he doing for us *now*?

In a complex and challenging world, many of those who trust in Jesus aren't sure what to truly believe. They see the news but not the Savior. They're caught between two devastating lies about God's ability to provide in modern times.

On one side are those who believe the lie that they've been abandoned. Many Christians have shut down and stopped trying to reconcile the idea of a loving God with a difficult world. Feeling left out, unloved, and unprovided for, they leave the church and the God who they think has not kept up his end of the bargain. Today almost 60 percent of those who grew up in the Christian church will leave it—and may give up their faith all together—within the first decade of their adult life.[5]

Even those who stay in the pews often mentally give up on God's promises of provision. They live as functional agnostics, *hoping* God is real but not really *believing* he actually makes a tangible difference in their day-to-day lives. *Sure,* they think, *God can handle the universe, but either he doesn't care or he can't be bothered to help me get a car that doesn't break down.* They trust the laws of economics more than the promises of Jesus and government programs more than God's people. And when those don't work, they're left with only scarcity and isolation.

On the other side of the Christian faith spectrum is another lie, which is just as insidious and damaging. The shiny, shallow promises of what's known as prosperity theology draw the wishful thinking of the disheartened and afraid. Prosperity speakers, including many who call themselves ministers of the gospel, tell believers it is their *right* to be blessed and it is God's *obligation* to provide. They portray him as an omniscient ATM that is accessed by a "positive confession" of faith. Humans can speak things into existence, and God orbits us. If we do things "right," then health, wealth, and power will be ours. (If we don't receive what we want, then we must be doing something wrong. Either way, the prosperity gospel preacher gets to keep our donated money.)

When that attitude of entitlement doesn't work—and I'm here to tell you it doesn't—weary Christians are left disillusioned and even disconnected from the God of Scripture.

But what if I told you there's another way to look at the place where our fear challenges our faith? A path that cuts between the two lies and leads to genuine, future-facing hope? God is not limited, after all, by our false beliefs and costly lies. He has a better way.

Finding the Pattern of Provision

Think about Genesis 1, of God hovering over the deep, speaking things into existence. It boggles my mind that God created hundreds of billions of galaxies, likely more than twenty per person currently living on earth.[6] God created, with a few simple words, the sun and sky, mountains and meadows, fish and flowers.

And what else did he create? That's right—us. Out of the dust of the earth, he created humans with five senses and a playground of experiences to explore. Did you know the human tongue contains more than ten thousand taste buds or that they are regenerated and replaced every two weeks, just so we can experience flavor in what we eat? Or that the human eye can see more than ten million colors?

This makes me wonder, *If God, in his generosity, creativity, and abundance, chose to create humans with such intricate detail, why do we doubt he has the capacity to care for a single person? Does his provision cover seemingly irrelevant and useless things, like a bunch of stars millions of miles out of reach, but not the very beings he created in his own image?*

When we try to argue that God doesn't care or we put him in a box we "control," we ignore the truth about his character. It's a mistake to write off God, believing he doesn't care about the details of either an individual life or the world as a whole. And it's a mistake to try to "control" life without him.

When we don't trust that God wants to provide for both our spiritual and our physical needs, we're left with only those two lies: scarcity thinking or the prosperity gospel. Instead of God's provisions, we turn to government. Instead of Scripture, we look to human ingenuity. Instead of calling on the power of a loving, sovereign God, we rely on ourselves.

We're disappointed when those efforts aren't enough, when we aren't enough. But the truth between the lies is that we were never meant to be enough on our own. God loves us and desperately wants a relationship with us. In fact, he demonstrated that love in full public view—on a cross. He woos us to trust him. He beckons us to draw near to him and he will draw near to us. He promises that he is a rewarder of those who diligently seek him.

We can understand these statements "draw near" and "diligently seek" as part of the rhythm of our relationship with God. Throughout this book, we will explore this rhythm, this pattern, to access what he has already provided. When we enter this rhythm, we are unlocking his promises, which are a de facto guarantee as he says, "Draw near to me, and I will draw near to you."

However, when we remove God from the world, our resulting false faith in self-sufficiency causes us to misunderstand our own limitations. What will set us free from this culture of not enough isn't more money, more time, or more security.

Getting that $10,000 I wished for didn't change my life. But I started something else that same year I wrote the "10 Rules of Alexander," and it has grown into a different list—a set of four principles that illustrate the rhythm of our relationship with God and eventually silenced my fear and answered my sense of scarcity.

These four principles are the guarantee of the abundance God was offering all along.

Jesus said, "I have come that they may have life, and that they may *have it more abundantly*" (John 10:10 NKJV, emphasis added). This path of truth takes us past the two lies of scarcity thinking and faulty prosperity theology. In the following chapters, we will follow this path together toward true abundance—perhaps not the way you have thought about it in the past but the way God promises will fill your every need today.

Hungry People on a Hill

Jesus said we must become like children to enter his kingdom (see Matthew 18:3). Over and over, we hear stories of children like Jaden who, through courage and pure goodness, seem to get closer to the kingdom of God than most disillusioned adults can today.

Jaden's story ultimately reminds me of another boy. This child's name has been lost to history, yet his gift is recorded not once but four times in the Bible. He too found his way past his own scarcity and into God's abundance.

To understand how important this boy's actions were, though, we need to start with a little bit of context. The story of Jesus's life, ministry, and resurrection is told four times in the New Testament, in four separate Gospels written by four different authors. Each book is full of examples of how Jesus met the physical needs of those around him. Every Gospel contains stories of Jesus healing the blind and welcoming the outcasts. Yet only one miracle, prior to the resurrection, appears in all four books, which underscores its importance.

After hearing of John the Baptist's death, Jesus retreated to a place of solitude. We don't know how long he was alone there, but eventually the disciples went to find him. Jesus's reputation was spreading, and crowds from across the region followed them into the remote wilderness. The Scriptures say Jesus felt compassion for the crowds as he witnessed their need. He set aside his own grief and engaged with the people. He taught them, healed them, and inspired them.

Five thousand men were in attendance that day, and most scholars estimate the entire crowd, including women and children, could have been closer to fifteen thousand people. Seeing such a multitude, Jesus said to the disciples, "Give them something to eat" (Matthew 14:16; Mark 6:37; Luke 9:13).

The book of John goes on to say that Jesus pulled Philip aside and asked, "Where shall we buy bread for these people to eat?" (6:5). Philip, standing right next to the Son of God but still trapped in the rules of human economics, answered, "It would take more than half a year's wages to buy enough bread for each one to have a bite!" (v. 7).

An unnamed disciple suggested they send the people away to find food and shelter in the neighboring towns. His message was clear: let someone else take care of the need; we've already done enough. On the surface, the disciple's reaction makes sense. The disciples were grasping for solutions in trying to care for the unexpected crowd. But you can also hear the guardedness, fear, and scarcity mentality in the suggestion. Yes, they had seen Jesus heal an individual person here and there. A lame man walked. A leper's skin cleared up. But this? Thousands of people were pressing in all around them. Fifteen thousand empty bellies were growling. Surely not even Jesus had enough to handle this situation.

Another disciple, Andrew, brought a new twist to the story: he found a boy, the child whose name has been lost to history, with five loaves and two fish. That might have been a generous dinner for one person, or perhaps the child was carrying a meal for his family, but what could so little do for thousands of people? How could something so small possibly be enough?

But the Son of God accepted what he was given without recorded comment. He instructed the crowd to sit. Then he took the food, and he blessed it, broke it, and gave it.

And all the people ate.

The people of first-century Israel, like the people of today, lived with scarcity and fear. For centuries, God's chosen people struggled to survive against oppressive and often murderous enemies. By the time of Jesus's birth, they were ruled by a violent Roman government that denied both their God and their traditions. The Jewish people were heavily taxed and strictly ruled. Famine was often a problem. And so it's even more miraculous that the Gospels tell us they ate that day until they were full. And not only that, but twelve baskets were left over.

All from a single lunch.

No wonder the story is included in each Gospel. That Jesus cared enough about the curious crowds of people to meet their physical needs with abundance illustrates the true nature of his message—in relation not only to the promise of eternal provision in heaven but also to his concern for their practical provision on earth.

The same is true for us today. When we're faced with an antagonistic society, a lack of resources, and a deep sense of insecurity and uncertainty, Jesus's miracle on the hillside offers insight into God's abundant provision.

Throughout this book, we will take a detailed look at what Jesus did that day. We will break his miracle into four distinct actions—what Brueggemann calls the "four decisive verbs of our sacramental existence"[7]—and then see how they reflect the rhythmic relationship between God and his creation. In this relationship, God gives us his provision, which covers us in even the most frightening times of not enough and protects us from the devil's most convincing lies.

Jesus *took* the bread, he *blessed* it, he *broke* it, and he *gave* it. This pattern draws us into a rhythm of relating to our Creator. This rhythm involves our faith and his response to it. In this book, we will walk through this rhythm together. Watch God work and provide for you!

1. He takes (we discover capacity)

   When Jesus took the loaves and fish and looked to heaven, he saw potential that no one else saw. Jesus saw not only the need of the people but also the *capacity* of the bread and fish. In part 1 of this book, we will explore how to understand and recognize the capacity God has placed in each of us, in others, and in his creation. We will see how capacity, which is based on God's purposes and glory, teaches us to look beyond our own "potential" to see the eternal and limitless provisions concealed in creation.

2. He blesses (we consecrate, invite him in)

Jesus took the loaves and fish and blessed them, dedicating them to God's higher glory. Jesus consecrated a simple meal and made it something that filled both a physical and a spiritual need. Consecration means "to make something holy or to set apart."[8] I have heard it described as to imbue with vitality. In part 2, we will explore what it means to consecrate what we have—however big or small it seems to us at the time—to God. We will look at what it means to invite him not just into our spiritual lives but also into our daily lives—our assets, debts, work, families, and even weaknesses. When his holiness, presence, and power come into our one-dimensional lives, something powerful happens.

3. He breaks (he reorders our lives through challenges)

Jesus did not hesitate to physically break the bread and fish after they had been consecrated . . . just as he does not hesitate to metaphorically break us from time to time. A consecrated life is usually not a perfect or easy one. Life throws us into wilderness experiences—death, disease, job loss, family problems. These painful and difficult events lead us to places of seeming loss and scarcity. Yet God resides in the wilderness, just as he resides in the hospitable places. In part 3, I will share some of my own darkest times so we can see, together, how being broken can reorient us and help us gain perspective. We will see how miracles often follow painful times. Challenges test our deepest faith, but if we are in the wilderness, we are also in the place to find a new perspective on abundance and the provision of eternity.

4. He gives (he provides, often through community)

Jesus gave others the loaves and fish to distribute. The miracle of the boy's lunch could have been stopped in its tracks if the disciples, or the crowd closest to Jesus, had refused to participate. Authentic provision happens when we form communities that represent the body of Christ through serving one another. Jesus meets us as we let go of our own desires and selfishness and instead focus on how to love the people in our lives, even those who seem unlovable. Abundance and selfishness are irreconcilable. In part 4, we will explore how feelings of scarcity appear when we don't see our role as God sees it—in which every sacrifice becomes an investment in the community.

If you have spent much time reading the New Testament, these actions might seem familiar to you. In fact, five stories in the New Testament reflect this same pattern (see sidebar "God's Pattern of Provision: Five New Testament Examples").

Through four simple and profound actions, Jesus shows us we are cared for. Remembering this can guide us throughout our lives. The remainder of this book is devoted to exploring how these acts interact and reflect the rhythmic nature of our relationship with God, in which we seek him and he always offers his provision.

God's Pattern of Provision: Five New Testament Examples

Sometime after Jesus performed the miracle of the five loaves and two fish, the Gospels of Matthew and Mark record a second, curiously similar situation. Once again, Jesus was in the wilderness, surrounded by crowds. He taught them, healed them, and served their community. Then Matthew 15:32 says Jesus told his disciples, "I have compassion for these people; they have already been with me three days and have nothing to eat. I do not want to send them away hungry, or they may collapse on the way."

Now keep in mind this was after these men, Jesus's closest companions, had watched him feed fifteen thousand people with nothing more than a sack lunch. And yet they didn't believe! Verse 33 says they asked, "Where could we get enough bread in this remote place to feed such a crowd?" a question that's uncomfortably familiar. Lord, why do you again ask us to do the impossible?

Sometimes our doubts are bigger than our memories.

Jesus responded, of course, with provision and love. He took what food was available—in this case, seven loaves and "a few small fish"—and gave thanks, broke, and shared. Again, there were baskets full of leftovers.

The third story is Jesus's last supper with his disciples (see Matthew 26:26–28; Mark 14:22–24; Luke 22:19–20). As the hour of his death neared, Jesus took the bread and the wine. He gave thanks and blessed them. He broke the bread and shared it with his closest friends. His previous miracles provided physical abundance, but his actions here filled the disciples' spiritual needs and prepared them emotionally for the coming trials. And there were trials. An arrest. A crucifixion. A burial. And then an empty tomb.

The fourth story is recorded in Luke 24. As two of Jesus's followers walked glumly away from Jerusalem on the morning of the third day after his death, Jesus himself came and walked with them. The believers did not recognize him, though, even as he unpacked the words of the prophets and explained why the Messiah had to suffer. It was only when they gathered for a meal that the miracle happened. "When he was at the table with them, he took bread, gave thanks, broke it and began to give it to them. Then their eyes were opened and they recognized him, and he disappeared from their sight" (vv. 30–31).

If that isn't enough, God gives us one more example of how four seemingly normal actions reflect his abundant provision. In Acts 27, we read how the apostle Paul was a prisoner of the Roman government, packed onto a boat for the dangerous crossing to Rome for trial. The voyage went horribly wrong, and the ship was caught in a storm that lasted for more than fourteen days. The crew was terrified, but Paul assured them they would live. An angel had visited him in a dream and told him so. He encouraged them to eat, and "after he said this, he took some bread and gave thanks to God in front of them all. Then he broke it and began to eat" (v. 35). The next morning they ran the ship aground on a sandy beach and were saved.

With such a long tradition, it's no surprise that today most Christian churches repeat all four steps Jesus took during the Last Supper in their practice of communion, in memory of Jesus's death and resurrection. It is a means of grace and a preview of the time when we will actually eat and drink at the banquet table in heaven.

Surely something that is repeated in Scripture five times is worth paying attention to. This is the four-step pattern of provision that inspired the book. Each time, God provided physically or spiritually, offered a deeper knowledge of himself, or rescued someone. Every step is rooted in God's promises. It is why I call this book *The God Guarantee*.

Part 1

CAPACITY

He directed the people to sit down on the grass. *Taking the five loaves and the two fish and looking up to heaven*, he gave thanks and broke the loaves. Then he gave them to the disciples, and the disciples gave them to the people.

Matthew 14:19, emphasis added

1

The Land of What Could Be

Understanding Capacity

I became a Christian when I was twenty-six years old. My mother, who was not a believer, was deeply concerned. "Do you really believe Jonah lived inside a fish for three days and survived?" she would quiz me. "Do you really think Noah and a boat full of animals survived a global flood?"

She feared I'd become a religious fanatic—the kind who believed in miracles and other crazy things.

In the spirit of Albert Einstein—a Jewish scientist and hardly a religious fanatic—either everything is a miracle or nothing is a miracle.[1] And when we look at the world around us, it's easy to see what he meant. Indeed, miracles happen every day, all around us.

When we walk on the beach and feel the sand beneath our toes, we rarely consider that we are stepping on the second most abundant element on earth—silica. It has existed for as long as the earth has had dry land, but only in the past few decades have people discovered some of what it can do. When silica is purified, made into ingots, and then sliced into wafers, it can be manufactured into microchips and semiconductors. These chips become the "brains" of our laptops, our smartphones, our cars, and, more and more often, even our homes.

If you had told my mother thirty years ago that she could carry a device in her pocket that could hold thousands of songs, send messages to someone on the other side of the world in seconds, and pinpoint her exact location using satellites floating far above the earth, making it almost impossible to ever get lost again, even she might have said, "It's a miracle!"

The Jerusalem Nano Bible, the smallest printed work ever, can fit on the head of a pin. Our cars will soon be driving themselves. But as amazing as human inventions are, it's the capacity God put into his natural creation that is beyond imagination.

I recently watched a video from author and USC professor Dr. Steven Shepard about the complexity of modern telecommunications. He explained with enthusiasm that the most reliable telecom network in the world today has only fourteen minutes of downtime annually. Fourteen minutes of downtime might sound good, until you consider the consequences that would have on certain other systems, like the human body. The average heart beats 2.5 billion times over more than seventy years. A fourteen-minute downtime in any one of those years, let alone *every* year, would likely be fatal.[2]

So is the human heart, which is so much more reliable and efficient than the most reliable systems created by humans, a miracle?

Aspirin was originally developed from the bark of a willow tree.[3] Scientists are using special genetic sequences found in sea urchins to formulate new responses to Alzheimer's disease

42

and cancer.[4] Penicillin comes from fungus.[5] Chronic high blood pressure is treated with a derivative of viper venom. The most common malignancy of childhood, acute lymphocytic leukemia, can be treated with a medicine derived from the Madagascar periwinkle. Five of the top ten prescription drugs have animal, plant, or microorganism origins.[6] Many more drugs come from plant-derived sources.

These things all seem pretty miraculous to me.

Wait a minute, you say. Turning sand into microchips or tree bark into medicine is a scientific process. It's not supernatural. Does it really fit the definition of a miracle?

You're right. Human developments must comply with the laws of science and nature—laws God established at creation.

Yet have you ever considered how intricate, how perfectly crafted, how *supernatural* those laws of science are? God created nature so precisely, and with so much prescience, that the billions of tiny pieces—all those galaxies and stars, all those cells in the heart, all those molecules of sand—work together year after year. Every generation uncovers more of the secrets and details provided for us at the beginning of time, divine solutions to meet all our needs.

When I think about the complexities all around us, and how much careful forethought went into each detail of nature, the only word I have to describe it is *miracle*.

And there's only One who can offer us the miracle of perfect provision.

Finding Capacity in Five Loaves and Two Fish

In Jesus's miracle of provision on the hillside, he began by *taking the bread and looking to heaven*. He didn't look at the people in the crowd, with their pressing needs and growing doubts. He didn't look to his disciples, who followed him but did not yet see the entire picture. He looked to God, the Creator of all that can be, and as a result, he saw not what this meager meal was but *what it could be.*

He saw the capacity of what he had been given.

Capacity is the fulfillment of opportunity God created in each thing and person for his purposes and glory. In God's provision, he makes the first move toward us, and he does so through creation. Being open to seeing this capacity in every person and thing is our response to his offer, creating the first aspect of the pattern of provision God offers to us.

Capacity may not be a word we use often, but we experience it every time we turn on one of those goal-driven reality TV shows that follow people who are losing weight, learning a new talent, or fixing up a house. We're drawn into the stories of renewal, wondering, *What could this become?*

Understanding the capacity God has put into every person and thing in the world takes that question one step further and makes us ask, What can I become?

We were each once a fertilized egg and then a newborn. In fact, our entire lives have been an unveiling of the potential capacity and life within us. And God is not through with that process. So we, like a child, need to have eyes of wonder to imagine the good work he has yet to complete in our lives and in the lives of others.

When I speak to groups or individuals about capacity, someone usually asks if it is the same as potential. That's a more familiar word today, used liberally by self-help folks and business consultants alike.

I choose to use capacity instead of potential because potential often refers to limited, tangible projects we explore without God's intervention. What I'm describing here is more than learning how to turn an unused closet into a mini media center or how to make the manufacturing process of a new product more profitable. Those ideas are based on human capabilities and are limited to what we can see and maximize with our human perspective.

Searching for potential, in other words, encourages people to be intuitive, not prayerful and open. Capacity, however, can be seen only with God's perspective, because it is based on his abilities and provision. Potential is always limited, but capacity is limitless. Understanding the difference is crucial.

A few years ago, I stood in a barren desert near the Dead Sea in the West Bank and looked down at the ruins of Qumran, an ancient settlement near the caves where the Dead Sea Scrolls were found. Amid the ruins were the dry, cracked cisterns that used to provide the people with water. They were likely engineering feats in their day, a creative solution to the problem of unpredictable rainfall and an undependable water supply. They were a solution with a great deal of *potential*. But human potential is limited, and those vessels certainly wouldn't be reliable today. However, scattered all over the Judean countryside are natural springs that bring fresh, life-giving water to the surface of the earth, just as they have for centuries. The *capacity* in these natural springs is unlimited.

As I looked at the cisterns, I thought of Jeremiah 2:13, which says, "My people have committed two sins: They have forsaken me, the spring of living water, and have dug their own cisterns, broken cisterns that cannot hold water." All too often we find ourselves trying to fill our own holes and meet our own needs, with only our own limited abilities. Not surprisingly, they're rarely enough. We live as broken cisterns, and the only thing that can fill us is living water. God is the living water. When we try to build our own cisterns, eventually all we have are leaking piles of pottery and putrid water. But when God provides, his provision is eternal.

Looking Up

Years ago, the young son of one of my best friends showed an uncommon ability to play tennis. The child was winning tournaments, and coaches were starting to notice and ask about him. Many parents would see this as a blessing, but my friend did not seem enthusiastic when he described the situation to me. You see, he was a chaplain for the men's professional tennis circuit at the time and was friends with some of the world's top athletes. He had a unique perspective on the kind of intense investment, both physically and mentally, that would be required of the entire family for his son to succeed, and some parts of that concerned him. However, my friend also did not want to hold his son back from a place where God wanted to use him.

My friend prayed long and hard, sought the counsel of others, and finally felt God telling him that his son should pursue other directions. The boy was not called to follow the difficult path of becoming a professional athlete. He had the capacity to be great, but my friend, through prayer, understood that God would not use this capacity for his purposes or glory. The child grew up and now happily works in another occupation. He also has a solid relationship with the Lord.

This story illustrates a second point I want to make about capacity: it's discovered through seeking God's purposes and glory rather than our own. If we consider any opportunity with the ultimate goal of trying to maximize our own experience or outcomes, we are limited to what we can see as an end result. But if we are open to seeking the ultimate story that only God can tell, the one that honors him above all else, then we move into a place where every opportunity is a chance to further his kingdom.

Too many, including myself at times, go the "maximize potential" route without seriously inquiring of the Lord. Business leaders who lock into their own maximization mode and individuals determined to reach their human potential often become proud, arrogant, and self-reliant in the process. That is not what we're trying to uncover in this chapter.

It's challenging to start this book here, because capacity is one of the most difficult concepts to grasp in this modern, measured, data-driven age. Our culture has drilled into us the idea that if we can't see something, it's not real. That our resources are zero sum (whatever is gained by one person is lost by another). We're told over and over that miracles don't happen.

Capacity is about what God sees, which is so much bigger than even the most expansive human potential. Capacity is multidimensional, bringing together the intrinsic potential of all of creation under the banner of God's purposes and glory. Capacity is not all about us.

One reason it is so easy to fall into Satan's trap of a scarcity mind-set is that we rarely have time anymore to stop and appreciate all the blessings God has showered on us, all the capacity for blessing others he has placed within us.

It is increasingly difficult to have a Sabbath day of rest and spiritual renewal or a chance to consider what exists in that place beyond what we can physically see. But just because we stopped looking doesn't mean it stopped existing.

God shows us over and over the importance of *looking up*, or looking to heaven, to see what can be. In Psalm 121:1–2, David writes, "I lift up my eyes to the mountains—where does my help come from? My help comes from the LORD, the Maker of heaven and earth." In Daniel 4:34, after King Nebuchadnezzar had been humbled and driven to live like a wild animal, he "raised [his] eyes toward heaven, and [his] sanity was restored." Then, in John 3:14–15, Jesus says, "Just as Moses lifted up the snake in the wilderness, so the Son of Man must be lifted up, that everyone who believes may have eternal life in him."

Living within God's capacity changes the entire conversation. It's no longer about living in scarcity and whether we have enough, because in regard to God's purposes, everything we are and everything we have can be more.

The Land of What Could Be

As an adolescent, Jeremy Cowart regularly scored poorly on aptitude tests and was routinely told he was below average. According to his teachers and peers, it looked as if Jeremy would not do anything particularly notable, let alone extraordinary, with his life. "I can't do this" became his answer to everything. Yet every week his parents would encourage him with Philippians 4:13, breathing life over him by telling him that he "can do all things through Christ who strengthens [him]" (NKJV).

Jeremy discovered a love for drawing and painting. After college, he set out to be a graphic designer in Nashville, building his talent while working with local musicians and recording labels. Then one day a friend suggested he give photography a try, and Jeremy discovered a new well of capacity he'd never known was there.

An agent called him out of the blue, and before he knew it, Jeremy was photographing A-list celebrities and releasing popular social media apps for photographers. Ten years later, the *Huffington Post* named Jeremy "the most influential photographer on the Internet."[7] But Jeremy's real success doesn't come from being a photographer to the rich and famous.

Inspired by his faith and the idea that greatness should serve a greater purpose, Jeremy founded Help Portrait, mobilizing one hundred thousand photographers to offer free portraits to those less fortunate around the world. As a result, just days after Haiti experienced a catastrophic earthquake in 2010, Jeremy was invited to Haiti to capture the country's stories of hope and brokenness. In his "Voices of Haiti" photo essay, the people of Haiti display their thoughts and prayers on pieces of rubble. This project went on to adorn the hall of the United Nations. In 2011, Jeremy traveled to Rwanda with a documentary team to tell the stories of reconciliation and forgiveness in the decades since the brutal genocide there. And today he continues to be a voice for his generation, using crowdfunding and social media to gather community support for those in need.

This is capacity in the flesh. Jeremy was a young man who, inspired by his parents' words, sought God's purposes and glory above his own. He opened himself to God's perspective, which led him to serve people in crisis as well as in power.

And in return, God took Jeremy to a place where he could be more than he ever dreamed of, in a life that constantly, joyfully bears fruit for God's kingdom. Over and over, God takes people like Jeremy and uncovers a capacity we struggle to see by human standards. Even as others chant "you are lacking" and "there is not enough," God unlocks doors that seem invisible to human eyes.

So is it conceivable that something in your life right now might be more, or lead you to more, than you can see right now? That your situation has capacity you have not yet realized? What about the situations and needs of those around you? The parent behind you in the carpool line or sitting on the bleachers watching the sports game. The mechanic who works on your car. The barista who makes your double latte. God has built capacity into each interaction.

The paradigm of capacity helps us see beyond what I call the Land of What Is, which is where a scarcity-driven culture leaves us, and realize there is a Land of What Could Be that is rooted in faith and possibility. This new place is where we see the miracles of provision, where the capacity God has built in us, in others, and in creation pushes past the boundaries of what seems possible. Inventors and scientists look at the Land of What Could Be and uncover the gifts God left for us in his creation. Prayer warriors look at the Land of What Could Be and see the chance for healing, peace, and new beginnings. And you and I look at the Land of What Could Be and find the answers to the dilemmas that have been plaguing our sleep and tugging at our hearts.

When we try to see from God's perspective, we discover a land *exploding* with provision. The sovereign God of the universe is on our side, and no matter what happens in life, he is ultimately in control. God created us and has placed within our minds, bodies, and personalities capacity far beyond our comprehension.

Consider this: willow bark existed thousands of years before anyone thought to make it into aspirin. It didn't exist by accident, waiting for the right scientist to see its capacity. That bark was part of an expansive, creative, powerful plan.

There are no limits to what is possible in the Land of What Could Be. And when we take everything we have and all we are and look to God, with faith in his provision and a commitment to his plan, he will provide for us. He will show us something new—or something familiar in a new, redemptive way—over and beyond what we can see with our human eyes. Our faith unlocks and unleashes this capacity.

If Jesus could see that a single serving of bread and fish had the capacity to feed thousands, imagine what the entire universe holds. It is just waiting for us to unlock it in God's way and according to his timing.

Ground War versus Air War

When I talk about capacity, I want to be clear that I'm not encouraging anyone to ignore reality or fall victim to the idea that all we need to do is throw our money into the air (or into the collection envelopes that appear like clockwork from "ministers" promising wealth and prosperity in return). I am a businessman, tasked with day-to-day responsibilities as well as spiritual challenges, and I know God's promises of provision do not excuse us from our responsibility to be good stewards and careful observers of reality. In fact, in my experience, God's provision is bestowed most generously on those who have one foot firmly planted in reality, in the present, and one foot stretching forward in faith of what God can do in the future.

What does this look like? For the last fifteen years, I have worked with leaders of businesses and ministries that are going through periods of transition or financial hardship. As we step back and question every idea they have about their organizations, markets, competition, capital structures, and so on, the issues that emerge almost always fall into one of two categories.

The leaders do not see reality clearly. They have an idea but think they have a product. They have a product but do not have a business. They may not understand their competition or pricing. My favorite quote is from Max De Pree: "The first responsibility of a leader is to define reality."[8] Jim Collins said something similar: "Confront the brutal facts."[9] We can all lose sight of where we really stand.

The leaders have little vision. On the other side of the issue are leaders who are effectively managing the day-to-day operations but who don't have a vision for how their actions fit together. I use the analogy of a ground war versus an air war. Some people are so focused on "taking the next hill" (the ground war) that they lose sight of how that hill fits into the overall landscape (the air war).

My favorite part of working through these issues is when I ask the following questions:

- What would you do if you had unlimited capital?
- Whom would you hire if you could hire anyone?
- What strategic partners could you approach?

Question by question, step by step, I help them get past the Land of What Is and enter the Land of What Could Be.

Why do I tell you this? Because the same challenges that plague businesses and ministries in these times of fear and scarcity are also affecting individuals, even Christians. Too many of us are paralyzed by our daily routines, lulled into complacency by the media's steady stream of gloom-and-doom messages and the marketplace's suggestion that the solution can be found only by spending more money. We follow all the rules, we sit obediently in the pews, but we forget why we're doing it all.

Emotionally trapped by what appear to be insurmountable obstacles, many let go of the faith that could draw them past themselves. They allow uncertainty about where the next rent payment will come from or the pressure of getting the kids into the right program to scream over faith's gentle and steady promise of a future of provision.

Faith and Wisdom

According to Hebrews 11:1, "faith is confidence in what we hope for and assurance about what we do not see." Verse 6 says that "without faith it is impossible to please God, because anyone who comes to him must believe that he exists and that he rewards those who earnestly seek him." God's miracle of provision rewards and provides for us as we act in accordance with what we hope for in the future based on "what we do not see."

Faith leads us to recognize the capacity of something, not just things on the surface.

Living in faith as well as in wisdom means leaning in to the unknown and being willing to take risks. The paralyzing thing about fear is that it makes us hold on and not engage. Prayerful risk-taking pleases God. Just as Jesus took the boy's bread and fish and looked to heaven, we need to take what we have in our lives—our time, energy, and resources—and prayerfully ask how God can use them.

In Mark 6:5–6, Jesus "could not do any miracles [in his hometown]. . . . He was amazed at their lack of faith." About his return, Luke 18:8 says, "When the Son of Man comes, will he find faith on the earth?" Faith seems to be the missing commodity. It is the key to entering the Land of What Could Be.

Faith is about trusting God and loving others. Faith focuses on the future, while wisdom brings prudence, measure, and thoughtfulness to our present circumstances. Faith shows us God has a purpose for a young man in Nashville, no matter what others say. Wisdom points him to both an art school education and mentors who can help him learn how to manage a business.

A constructive tension is necessary between the here and now (the Land That Is) and the future (the Land of What Could Be). A life based only on the future can trap us in a world of false promises and emotions that are not guided by wisdom. A life bound in the limited observation of the present can cut us off from the unexpected blessings that come from trusting God's most remarkable and counterintuitive plans for us. We need to root ourselves firmly in both to experience his full provision.

Without wisdom, we cannot recognize the false prophets who hijack the faith narrative, making it about them and their ministry rather than about God and his capacity. Through diligence we learn to doubt those who reduce faith to a series of actions, usually donations, they guarantee will elicit a specific response from God. Their actions fail to pass our standards of wisdom, because their promises are devoid of a relationship with God or others. They are arrogant, as they encourage others to rely on them, not God, for guidance. They stand between us and the capacity God has for us.

God's promise of provision is not a promise that if we have enough faith we will get everything we want, or even everything we think we need. His capacity is not a guarantee of personal success and a peaceful, easy, or stress-free life. As we'll see in the next chapter, sometimes we find our true capacity only in times of stress and scarcity.

God's Challenge to Each of Us

The Old Testament originally put forward 613 laws that God's people were supposed to follow. Moses summarized and narrowed those down to the Ten Commandments. The prophet Micah reduced those to three commands: do justice, love mercy, and walk humbly with your God (see Micah 6:8). And then, as Jesus brought us out of the law and into the new covenant, he reduced them to two: love God with all your heart, soul, mind, and strength (see Matthew 22:37; Mark 12:30; Luke 10:27), and love your neighbor as you love yourself (see Matthew 22:39; Mark 12:31; Luke 10:27). "All the Law and the Prophets," Jesus said, "hang on these two commandments" (Matthew 22:40).

Dozens of books and thousands of sermons have been written on Jesus's words—and on every nuance of meaning

Jesus put into them. Yet recently, as I was working on the idea for this book, I realized something I'd never noticed before.

Both of Jesus's supreme commands are about continuously expanding and building our capacity to love. Just as athletes' physical capacity grows as they train regularly, our capacity to love grows as we love. There is no limit to how much God calls us to love.

We are called to love God with *all* our being, to fill ourselves completely with our dedication to him. And we are told to see others as we see ourselves—that is, to see others as just as central to our experience as we are. The more we put others—their needs, feelings, and desires—at the same level of importance we put ourselves, the more God expands our capacity, deepening our connection to him.

God will provide for us as we recognize and help others reach their fullness and capacity in Christ. He will also bless us in ways we cannot imagine on our own. There is something holy about seeing someone else's capacity, articulating it, and becoming part of the journey to discover it. As we acknowledge that God creates each person to be something more than they may see or feel right now, and as we understand the capacity he has built in others, his creation, and us, we discover his provision.

Henry Scougal says, "The worth and excellency of a soul is to be measured by the object of its love."[10] A generous spirit and a willing heart are key messages in the New Testament. God desires for his love to compel those who love him to outserve, outhonor, and outlove one another. There's no holding anything back with this kind of love, no place for a scarcity mind-set of protecting what's "mine" in fear of the future.

"Freely you have received; freely give," Jesus told his disciples as he sent them out to minister to those who had physical and emotional needs (Matthew 10:8). Paul pushed the Roman Christians to "be devoted to one another in love. Honor one another above yourselves" (Romans 12:10). Later, to the Corinthians, he said, "I want to test the sincerity of your love by comparing it with the earnestness of others" (2 Corinthians 8:8).

Does the God of love really compare the devotion and actions of his children? Paul clearly said he does in the areas of love, sincerity, and honor.

These verses struck me right between the shoulder blades in the early years of my marriage. Lisa and I were young, and a series of financial challenges and unexpected needs had depleted our bank accounts and left us in a place that felt unstable. But then I received my first-ever bonus at work—a check for $5,000. After a year of so much bad news, this money would make such a difference!

I immediately started planning how we would spend it. I took Lisa and the boys out to Wendy's for hamburgers and fries (our version of splurging in those days) and told them the good news.

Lisa's eyes lit up. "That's so exciting!" she said. "You'll never believe what happened today."

"What happened?" I asked.

"I got a letter from Nancy." Our friend Nancy was a missionary nurse working among the desperately poor in Sudan. "She needs to buy a jeep so she can serve her patients. And guess how much she needs?"

My heart sank. "Five thousand dollars?" I asked.

"Five thousand dollars," Lisa confirmed.

I didn't want to do it. We *needed* that money. I had *earned* that money. But I looked at Lisa, who was already so confident of what we should do, and I realized the boys were watching us. I needed to set a good example. As I tried to wipe the look of shock from my face, Lisa said, "Jack, will you pray about it?"

"Of course I will."

That evening as I prayed, God showed me the thousands of Sudanese children and adults who would receive inoculations and emergency care because of that jeep. I saw how Grace would use it to save lives.

God used that bonus to introduce me to the Land of What Could Be. He replaced my reluctance with a sense of privilege that he had chosen our family to take part in his work. That bonus check didn't help us pay for the things I thought we needed; instead, it became a reminder that God's economy is an economy of abundance, not scarcity. I had planned to use God's blessings for my family and myself. But God wanted me to channel them to others in ways bigger than I could have imagined.

Are you willing to put your God and your neighbor above your comfort? Above your house, your big-screen TV, your child's college savings account, and your image of what your life *should* look like?

Later, in part 4, we will spend more time exploring the connection between God's provision and his expectations of us, as his creations, to fully love and care for one another. For now, I want to emphasize that living in God's capacity and provision isn't a gift that comes without any expectations. The Bible calls us over and over to live as selfless and faithful reflections of the example he set for us.

If a farmer wants to have a harvest in the fall, he can't simply rely on God's gifts of soil, rain, and sun to do all the work. For the best results, the farmer must do his part. He must plow the field, plant the crop, and then tend it while it grows. Likewise, if we want to see the full abundance of God's provision in our lives, we can't just rely on God to do all the work. We also have a part to play.

Most evangelical churches like to focus more on the "grace" aspect of our relationship with God than the "work" part of it. Work sounds too much like there's a list of rules we have to follow to get into heaven, an idea that is distinctly outside the Christian narrative.

But as Dallas Willard puts it so well, "Grace is not opposed to effort, it is opposed to earning."[11] We are saved through grace, and our eternal lives are secured only through the love and redemption God offers freely. But that moment of salvation is just the beginning of a much bigger, deeper relationship.

The healthiest marriages, when considered over time, are a dance of both giving and receiving. Because of the deep love and respect between the partners, each offers their best to the other, serves the other, and receives the sacrifice of the other. Our relationship with God is similar. Christ died for us so that we can live for him. We receive his salvation, and this ideally creates a relationship that is so deep we want to offer our best to him in return.

If you talk to a competitive athlete, they will tell you that only through consistent, incremental training does their capacity increase. Few runners finish a marathon the first time they ever lace up their shoes and set out to run. Perhaps at first they can run only a mile or two before they have to stop, winded and sore. But by steadily, consistently pushing their boundaries, they add distance. Their capacity increases.

As we practice loving with *all* of ourselves, giving ourselves fully to living out Jesus's commandments, we expand our capacity to love. The more we love, the less our circumstances can be driven by fear and isolation.

There is no limit to what God can provide when we let go and love with everything we have. When we learn to take our time, energy, and resources and look up to God's purposes rather than being dragged down into the narrow perspective of a hurting world, we enter the Land of What Could Be. We discover the capacity God created in us and in others. We learn to seek his purposes and his glory, and doing so expands our capacity to love and give.

God's Rhythm of Provision for You: Capacity

Think for a minute about the capacity God put in beach sand. It can be used to make concrete or the brains of a smartphone. God loves you and has built so much capacity in you to grow, learn, and create. He also can bring new people and circumstances into your life.

Are you stuck in the Land of What Is? Are the pressures so great that you find yourself "walking by sight" rather than believing in God's perfect plan for you? Say a short prayer to begin this journey of provision. Think of seeds of capacity you have in your life that you may not have focused on. Ask him to open a new door for you this month.

Throughout this book, you will be able to evaluate how you are doing. In the area of capacity, where would you place yourself on a scale of 1 to 10?

1 I am totally overwhelmed in every way. I am stuck in the Land of What Is. I have a hard time believing in God or in his promises.

5 My life is up and down. I seem to do well, believe in God, then circumstances knock me down and I lose faith.

10 I walk with God. I stumble at times but normally believe in his love and provision for me.

Your score: _____

Enter your score on page 211. After filling in all your scores, you will have a total score and receive access to a free, nationally recognized short film to encourage you. If you are reading an electronic book, you can access an assessment at www.thegodguarantee.com/ebook.

2

A Time to Plant

Capacity in Times of Fear and Scarcity

I wonder what the disciples thought as they watched Jesus holding the loaves and fish. There wasn't much there. Did they think he'd just acquired lunch for their inner circle, the followers who were most worthy? Were they tempted to reach out and take their share? After all, they'd been working hard all day—and for weeks and months before this. These crowds were just here for the day, but the disciples had been there for the duration, and they were hungry. Surely Jesus would see that *they* deserved to be blessed before anyone else.

Of course, that's not what happened, but it's easy to miss the scale of God's capacity, and the infinite opportunities of his provision, in times of scarcity and need.

Most Christians, if asked, will say they believe God is capable of greater things, and bigger perspectives, than we are. But then the rubber meets the road, as the saying goes.

Those student loans aren't going to pay themselves. Your aging parents will need care soon and your son just made the all-state travel team and your new boss expects you to work more hours and your calendar is a rainbow of obligations—each one a need that tugs at your heart. God may be omniscient and all-powerful, but in your experience, you're the only one who's going to take care of you.

"God helps those who help themselves" becomes the armor of those who feel fragile and limited. "No one else is going to help us, so no one else should expect our help." Instead of relying on God's capacity for physical and spiritual provision, we fall back on our own limited human potential. And then, when it's not enough, we shake our fists and say, "I told you so! I knew I should have held on tighter!"

That's exactly what the enemy wants us to think.

Satan's Capacity Killers

Christians like to talk about how God has a narrative, a story that will eventually lead us to the Promised Land of milk and honey. But in recent years, less attention has been paid to the truth that there is also a counternarrative, a story that pushes us into the darkest corners of despair and hopelessness.

There is a Father, but there is also an enemy.

The enemy, Satan, is real. First Peter 5:8 tells us, "Your enemy the devil prowls around like a roaring lion looking for someone to devour."

He will do everything to distract you, hurt you, and make you believe there is not enough. That *you* are not enough. He will attack you in the places where you are most vulnerable. He will make empty promises of future satisfaction and fulfillment. He will brew dissatisfaction in your soul and blatantly lie to you about God's love and provision.

Jesus warned us about Satan. "When anyone hears the message about the kingdom and does not understand it, the evil one comes and snatches away what was sown in their heart" (Matthew 13:19).

God created us to learn, grow, and be all that we can be in him. Satan wants the opposite. He loves nothing more than to see people not reach their fullness and capacity. Thwarting our opportunities means thwarting the fullness of God's plans for us and our communities, so Satan will use whatever points of weakness he can find, especially our own fears, to hold us back.

I see Satan's hand in the statistics that say the majority of adult Americans are obese or 75 percent of people receiving food stamps are functionally illiterate.[1] How can that be? Our infrastructure can bring healthy food to the most remote corners of the country, and the US national education system spends more than $12,000 per student per year, more than almost any country in the world. The media may blame societal failings, and some Christians point their fingers and blame immoral behavior, but I see these as signs of a deeper spiritual battle going on for our bodies and our minds—those intricate creations God designed to be more reliable than supercomputers and telecom networks. Every time the enemy robs us of our capacity to grow and live, he wins.

Satan has a whole arsenal of these capacity killers. Debt and oppressive tax systems strip our incomes and limit our future capacity. Addictions to everything from nicotine to junk food steal our physical health, shorten our life spans, and enslave us to an increasingly controlling obsession.

Gambling and lotteries undermine the American work ethic and the belief that reward comes from hard work and effort. Pornography creates a false reality and undermines healthy relationships.

If those don't tempt you, Satan has another set of capacity killers we don't hear as much about from the pulpit. Materialism causes us to spend our time and resources on the idolatry of things and a never-ending comparison trap with others. Self-righteousness separates us from our communities, tempting us to judge instead of offer compassion. Electronic gadgets and entertainment devices, when overused, draw our attention away from our families and personal spiritual growth.

All capacity killers lead us away from experiencing the fullness of blessing that God has for us.

Every day is a battle. The enemy knows exactly where your weak spots are, and he will use them to distract you and build distance between you and your community. He'll tell you that God wants you to take care of yourself first. That you must protect what you have for your children. That someone with fewer responsibilities or better health or different skills will be more adept at doing whatever God is tugging at your heart to do.

"God doesn't really expect you to love that person," the enemy whispers. "Look at their ungodly choices, their mistakes, their lifestyle. Surely God doesn't want you to spend your hard-earned free time or resources on them. What have they ever done for you?"

These capacity killers, and hundreds more, drive us to places of lack and despair. They distract us into seeing only ourselves, stopping us from taking what we have to the Land of What Could Be.

Unless we can see with eyes of faith the capacity God has given, we will succumb to the snares of the enemy that seek to rob us of God's provision in our lives.

God wants us to sow and be generous. Satan wants us to be fearful and hold on to what we have.

Only the Planted Seed Bears Fruit

In the last chapter, we talked about the importance of the farmer's role in creating a harvest. But not long ago, I read an article about a completely different approach toward seeds.

Deep within a mountain on an island in Svalbard, Norway, not far from the North Pole, the Svalbard Global Seed Vault is trying to provide a "fail-safe" safety net to prevent the accidental loss of diversity in traditional gene banks. Governments from around the world have sent more than 860,000 samples of prized varieties of crops and species, which are sealed in subfreezing temperatures and low humidity. This "bank" and several others like it around the world exist to protect the human race in the event of natural disasters or other cataclysms.

On the surface, the goal of being the "ultimate insurance policy for the world's food supply" is admirable. However, things are often more complicated than they appear. Critics have expressed concerns that storing these seeds, without using them, is not the best way to preserve a species. Phil Pardey, an agricultural economist, states, "All they are doing is parking the seeds" and not testing them for useful traits.[2] Do they have built-in resistance to scourges, pests, or droughts? Could they survive in the modern world? We don't know. In fact, some of the older seeds may have already lost their viability. Some experts argue that planting seeds in diversified places around the world and letting them grow and evolve to meet the needs of nature is a better way to preserve them.

To me, the seed bank concept is a clear example of what it means to live with a limited, scarcity-focused mind-set. It reminds me of Jesus's parable in Matthew 25:14–30 about the rich man who went on a journey, entrusting his servants with his money in his absence. On his return, he praised those servants who had taken risks to expand their master's kingdom; they had invested the gold and made more money. However, he was angry with the servant who had hidden the gold and been too afraid to use it.

The master had offered gifts to his servants, and when one wasted the offer, he disrupted the rhythm of the relationship. He took but did nothing with the gift. He put his seeds into a cold storage vault instead of entrusting them to the ground.

I'm not saying we shouldn't protect our planet's resources for the future. We are called to be wise stewards of God's creation, and I want my grandchildren's grandchildren to know the pleasure of a fresh ear of corn or a sun-ripened heirloom tomato. But this seems like a particularly poor way to get there. The seed vault is a scarcity-based solution, when God calls us instead to be both creative and strategic in using our gifts and harnessing our resources. Planting seeds in diverse places around the world seems to be a wiser approach. Jesus himself said that "unless a kernel of wheat falls to the ground and dies, it remains only a single seed. But if it dies, it produces many seeds" (John 12:24).

The enemy fills us with fear. He encourages us to protect our "seeds" of capacity, storing or hoarding them, cutting short

God's future provision. He whispers that we will never have another opportunity like this, another resource. He says that by allowing God to direct our future we are letting too much go. We see ourselves losing control of our seeds, wondering whether we will ever have more. Or we hesitate to plant, afraid the seeds might die and the outcome will not be what we want.

What if I take this chance and it fails? What if I try this but can't do it?

Satan drives us to allow fear, not faith, to guide us. But if we don't step out in faith and sow, then there will be no harvest to reap.

My friend Pastor Chip Ingram tells a story about when he and his wife were newly married. It was early in Chip's ministry, and there wasn't much extra money. They had a neighbor who was raising her young child alone after being abandoned by her husband. As rent came due one month, she confessed to Chip's wife that she did not have enough to pay the bill.

The Ingrams felt burdened for her, wanting to help, but they barely had enough money in the bank to pay their own rent. After much prayer, they decided to pay their neighbor's rent instead of their own. As Chip tells the story, he and his wife had no idea how they were going to make ends meet. Rent was due in three days, and they had only ten dollars in their bank account. On the third day, they received an envelope in the mail. It was from someone the Ingrams hadn't seen or talked to in years—a young man who had been blessed as a high school student by Chip's youth ministry. The man had been praying when he felt the Lord nudge him to send a check for the exact amount the Ingrams needed. God miraculously provided.[3]

The seeds aren't ours. God reminds us over and over that none of this—not our money, not our health, not our families—is really our own. Everything is his and is part of his divine plan. God's capacity for each of us is more than we can see; only by letting go of the limiting idea of human potential can we be part of his provision.

This, like so many things, was a truth I learned the hard way—and only over time. I've already told you I was driven as a young man to compete and succeed, believing I alone was responsible for meeting all my needs. I worked throughout my college years at Duke University, passed my CPA exam, and took a job at one of the most prestigious international accounting firms in the world. After six years of hard work, I was given one of the largest accounts our office handled. Every previous account manager had gone on to become a partner in the firm. This, I was sure, was my ticket to success and stability.

A notice went out to all my colleagues about this appointment, congratulating me on the promotion. I basked in the attention. But then, a few days later, a senior executive at the account called the managing partner at my firm. Long story short, he asked that I be removed from the account. He did not like me and wanted another manager to handle the business.

A second notice went out to the employees at my company, announcing another "new" account manager. I was assigned a small account that was not familiar or noteworthy to anyone.

I was humiliated. From my perspective, I'd been put on a path to failure.

But God had a different plan. I worked well with that small, relatively unknown firm, and as a result, the owner of the business, a wealthy European, hired me directly four years later. He and I eventually became partners in two businesses I ran successfully for many years.

Meanwhile, the global accounting firm I had worked for lost its way and went bankrupt in the Enron scandal. The partners at the firm—whom I'd held up as the pinnacle of professional success—lost their entire investments.

I'm not saying I was blessed for my behavior or those at my former firm were punished for theirs. But as I look at the span of my life and the things God has revealed, that experience is a beacon reminder that fortunes change in ways we don't expect. Only God can see the whole picture. Our job is to plant our seeds every chance we get and then let them germinate and grow while we diligently seek God's direction, even when we don't know the outcome.

Results May Vary

I love to hear stories like Chip Ingram's and to see the ways God has worked to bring about capacity I never could have imagined in my own life. But it's important to acknowledge that not every story has an ending like this.

God may call you to do something, but that doesn't mean the outcome will be what you want it to be or you will immediately see the blessings. Acting in faith means doing the right thing, even when it costs you something. Not every situation ends up with you receiving the rent money you've been called to give away, and not every new job brings a financial windfall.

Sometimes the lesson is not one of provision but of dependence. This topic is addressed more in-depth in part 3, where we discuss challenges.

Faithfully seeking God's capacity means being willing to take risks and acknowledge our lack of control. But *risk* is a scary word. The Land of What Is wants certainty; the people who live there think taking risks is somehow not being a good steward of what God gives us. I disagree. I believe prayerful risk-taking pleases God. Hebrews 11:6 says God will reward "those who earnestly seek him."

The key is to live in relationship with God and in tune to where he is leading us. Doing so will make us more willing to put everything, even the things that scare us, out on the table for him to use as he sees fit.

God will care and provide for us as we take faithful risks, but that isn't the same as saying we will materially benefit, or even break even, from every physical or emotional investment he leads us to make. God's guarantees come as we move forward, plant our seeds, and engage in service to others.

Learning to live with a view to God's capacity means we are conscious of the seeds he has planted within us, others, and his creation that can totally reframe any situation. Living this way is not a trick to force God to make us wealthy or to bless us in the ways we think we should be blessed. God's plans are much bigger than the most complicated scenario we can imagine; his concern for all of humanity is much deeper than anything we can fathom.

Something that really helped me with risk-taking is remembering that when I take risks and lose, *God doesn't lose*. Choosing to live in faith of God's capacity for provision means separating our thoughts about what's right—what we're called by God to do—from our instant personal gain and learning to see past the immediate outcome to the long-term purpose.

This has been an expensive lesson to learn. In 2010, a friend approached me about a medical patent he'd purchased that would be of great benefit to people in rural areas. The device separates blood and plasma and then dries them so the plasma can be shipped inexpensively to labs where diseases can be diagnosed and treated efficiently and inexpensively. I prayed about the situation, I talked to my family, and I sensed that God wanted me to make an investment in this fledgling company. I believed it could help millions of people receive better health care.

In the years since my investment, the patent's technology has been perfected, and it has attracted the attention of some of the biggest, most powerful companies in health care. However, the process took much longer than expected, and it is doubtful that, even with the sale of the patent, I will recoup my investment.

The mission of the kingdom of God will advance even if my financial investment is a loss. God didn't lose; he just shifted what was his from one pocket to another, to a place where it can do more good.

Or consider Steve, a local pastor here in Atlanta. One Sunday morning, just minutes after he'd finished a sermon on inviting vulnerable people into our lives, he and his wife spotted Rodney, a nineteen-year-old with a history of suicide attempts, lingering in the back of the sanctuary. Rodney had no family, and it appeared no one cared about him. Steve, who is Caucasian, approached Rodney, who is African American, and asked if he'd like to live with them and become part of their family. With a young family of their own, Steve and his wife were taking a risk fostering a troubled teen. Yet it was what they felt God was leading them to do.

And you know what? Life for the family wasn't perfect; there was conflict. Rodney stayed for a while but eventually moved out. He's in a better place emotionally and spiritually than he was, though, and Steve's family planted seeds that may bear fruit.

Steve and his wife were faithful to what God called them to do. And someday, when they face the eternal Master, they will be able to report that instead of burying what they'd been given, they invested it for his glory.

We don't always see the outcome of our actions, and committing to live in God's capacity doesn't mean we'll always have a happy ending worthy of a Hallmark movie. But his purposes—and his plan—are bigger than what we can see.

Called to Serve

One of our grandsons, Sam, was named after the Old Testament hero Samuel, whose mother dedicated him to the Lord. When Sam was born, he looked like a strong, healthy baby. Our family welcomed him with joy and had visions of him playing sports and roughhousing with his older brothers. But we found out a few days later that he had some very serious health issues. Sam needed open-heart surgery as an infant, but even then his journey was likely not over. We had no idea what was around the corner for Sam. Thankfully, he has overcome many of his early challenges and gives his siblings a run for their money.

Our family bonded together and prayed continuously for Sam during the scary time preceding his heart repair. One of the most meaningful moments I can remember happened during a conversation with my son John, Sam's father. After praying for Sam, he told me, "You always hear people ask, 'Why me?' when difficult or tragic circumstances arrive. But I am so glad that God chose our family for Sam. I can't imagine if he had been born to a family with no health insurance or to a single mom with no support network. We have the capacity to love him and help him be all he can be, but we are also blessed in that we need to rely on God to take care of Sam and we are doing just that." As he spoke, I had a new vision of how God could use this situation, and this beloved child, for his kingdom.

Looking past my own immediate worries to see God's capacity at work in the world around me is a lesson I've had to learn over and over. Having come from a childhood full of scarcity and fear, never believing there was enough money or love to fill the holes in my heart, I still struggle with the process of letting go and giving to others. But God's view of the world and his unfailing love give me a vision of the future based on hope. Living in his capacity has reoriented my thinking.

God calls each of us to our full capacity in different ways. Some are called to step out and lead; many of my closest friends have followed God's call to the pulpit or to the microphone of a ministry. Their capacity grows as they speak God's truth in both faith and wisdom. Others discover their capacity by being salt and light in the world. They serve in businesses, organizations, schools, homes, and workplaces across the country, open to God's calling to speak up, give generously, and serve others. Their capacity expands through personal relationships and the intimate service that happens when we invest ourselves in the lives of others.

I recently saw one of the most intimate, practical expressions of God's capacity for change in the life of our friend

Natasha. Lisa and I have known Natasha for more than twenty years, and she has shared many of her struggles with us during that time. She lost both of her parents at a young age and struggled with health issues and regular employment. The rest of her family had cut her off, and she hadn't seen them for more than ten years. She went to school and became a nurse's aide, but even then she lived under financial stress, burdened with significant health issues. Lisa would regularly pray with Natasha and ask for God's provision in her life.

A few months ago, Lisa felt called to do something to address one of Natasha's most visible challenges—her decaying teeth. They were affecting Natasha's health, self-confidence, and interactions with other people. Lisa works for Good Samaritan Health Center, which provides care for the poor and uninsured, in downtown Atlanta. She made a few calls and got Natasha in to see one of the dentists. After months of procedures, Natasha came to see us with a brand-new smile. With her new dentures came a new level of confidence. For the first time in years, she reached out to her estranged family, and they invited her to join them for the holidays. She also got a new job that provides a steady income.

And the changes all started with a nudge from God to reach out in love.

Where is God calling you to stretch yourself, to expand your capacity by showing love to others? For Lisa, it was making the connections to get a friend some needed dental care. For a little boy on a hillside, it was handing over his limited supply of food. For Jeremy Cowart, it was using his camera to humanize and bring light to some of the darkest stories. For the Ingrams, it was sharing their rent money. In each case, God called a person to take a risk and step into an adventure of experiencing God's capacity for provision. He showed them the answers and provisions that were already there—miraculously provided through the intricate work of his creation and just waiting to be prayerfully discovered.

In my experience, God regularly calls us to our passions, which often come from the places where we hurt. If you feel your heart being pulled toward a fatherless child or if your prayer time seems to keep turning to the victims of a recent tragedy, be open to hearing what God is calling you to do. How can you be part of his promise of provision for his other children? How will he bless your faithfulness in return?

If you are overwhelmed by how little you think you have, you may not see how your raw materials and gifts can be turned into more—how God can use you to be more. But the capacity is there; God's provision is just waiting for you to uncover it through prayer, diligence, and a willingness to actively and generously love others.

Uncovering your capacity often won't be easy. God will see capacity in places where your human perspective would never find it.

For example, have you ever really looked at the ocean? One of my favorite hobbies is deep-sea fishing, so I've spent many hours on the back of a boat, studying an endless stretch of water that can, at times, seem intimidating. On my earliest trips, I was baffled. How could I even begin to find a fish in the middle of so much space?

Fortunately, I had guides I could learn from. I watched as they put out six or seven lines, even if only two or three people were fishing. Each line had a different kind of rod, a different weight to change the depth, and a different bait or lure, all strategically chosen to attract various kinds of fish. The captain would turn on the underwater fish finder, which uses sonar to locate schools of fish by detecting pulses of sound energy. Our odds, I realized, of finding a tiny fish in a great big ocean were getting better and better. That endless stretch of water was turning into a measurable, predictable science.

Our quest for capacity is similar. We may look at the world, vast and seemingly full of need, and feel small and lost. Where can we even start to discover the purpose, satisfaction, and provision God promises? Like the fishermen, we need to take a logical approach, putting into practice the things we know: God desires for us to talk with him about the opportunities before us and to ask for eyes to see the things beyond the here and now. He calls us to be involved, obtain evidence, and be diligent.

Lifting our eyes in prayer reveals capacity.

Loving God and living within the rhythm of relationship build capacity.

Effort builds capacity.

Understanding our unique strengths and gifts builds capacity.

Serving in love builds capacity.

Making investments in faith builds capacity.

From "If" to "How Many?"

The logical approach of my fishing guides brought me from a place of wondering whether I would ever catch a fish to thinking, *I wonder how many we will catch today.* This pivot was critical to helping me enjoy fishing, and it's even more important for us in life. We overcome scarcity and fear when we get to a place where we throw out as many "lines" as we can and ask, *I wonder how many fish God will bring me?*

When we pivot from wondering "if" to "how many?" we move from a place of scarcity and fear to a place of faith and abundance.

The world today is focused on assessments and aptitude tests, which try to measure what is rather than what could be. But God's way is different. He directs us to places of purpose, service, fulfillment, and provision by calling us, in every season, to look at the Land of What Could Be. When we pivot from wondering *if* we will be provided for to wondering *how many* blessings God will give us, we stop seeing things just as they appear to be and start seeing the limitless capacity of our Creator. Hope is restored when we experience the freedom that comes from believing God is bigger than what we see. He can take the unredeemable and redeem them. He can make what is barren teem with life. God "does not change like shifting shadows" (James 1:17); he has everything under control.

As you look heavenward, ask God to prompt you regarding whom you can bless with your energy, time, giftedness, connections, and resources. Exercising your faith will actually build your capacity. It will also build the "muscle mass" of your faith.

Through faith, we see that God has already provided the seeds of provision in us, in others, and in his creation. The opportunities are close at hand, and now it's up to us to plant and care for them.

We have seen how a camera, a set of dentures, and even an unwelcome demotion all pointed toward future provision and purpose. We have seen how families discovered unexpected capacities for love and grace when they opened themselves to sharing their resources, their time, and even their homes. Embracing this idea of capacity sets you on an adventure of faith.

——God's Rhythm of Provision for You: Capacity Killers——

In chapter 2, you drew near to God and asked him for faith and to open new doors for you. Now think about the battle that is going on to steal your capacity. God created each of us with capacity beyond what we can imagine. Much of our future care and provision come from this capacity being unlocked. However, the pressures of this world make it easy for people to fall into alcohol or drug abuse; addiction to pornography, food, or gambling; or other harmful habits.

God is for you! However, you have an enemy who wants to steal, kill, and destroy. Say a short prayer for protection from this enemy, Satan, and ask God to take away your unhealthy desires. Share this prayer with a close friend.

In the area of capacity killers, evaluate how you are doing on a scale of 1 to 10:

① I am enslaved to one or more capacity killers. I have lost much of my hope that things can change.

⑤ I have had issues with capacity killers, and I still need help and support.

⑩ By God's grace, I am doing fine now.

Your score: _____

Enter your score on page 211.

Part 2

CONSECRATION

Taking the five loaves and the two fish and looking up to heaven, *he gave thanks* and broke the loaves. Then he gave them to his disciples to distribute to the people. He also divided the two fish among them all.

Mark 6:41, emphasis added

3

The Invisible Hand

Understanding Consecration

Hungry people covering a hillside waited, watching to see what would happen next. The Teacher's instruction to sit had spread through the crowd with a ripple of anticipation. They were hungry and tired.

But Jesus, it seems, didn't feel pressured to rush. He took his time as he held the boy's small contribution, looking to heaven to find its capacity. And then, we see in each of the Gospel accounts, he gave thanks.

This was no casual, routine "God is good, God is great . . ." blessing said before a meal. This was something much deeper, something that had the power to make food multiply.

I love the way Walter Brueggemann describes the meal as a "sit-down thanksgiving dinner that matches the needs of the people with the generosity of God." He continues:

His actions are transformative. The bread stays exactly what it is—bread—yet it becomes something it never was before: a carrier of all the hidden, powerful gifts of God. The crowd stays as it is, but it becomes something it never thought it would be: a people entitled to what they can't provide for themselves. The desert stays as it is, but it becomes something that no one would ever expect: a viable place of existence, the arena for the reign of God.[1]

When Jesus blessed the boy's lunch, he invoked God's presence, power, and holiness to do something with the offering. He *consecrated* it.

Consecration is a word that doesn't come up very often in the modern world, unless you're part of a church that schedules an annual "Consecration Sunday" to encourage greater financial commitment from its members. Some denominations also "consecrate" the bread and the wine in their communion services. But these uses of the word don't begin to capture the fullness of what consecration truly is—and what it can bring to our spiritual practices.

True consecration is an association with the sacred, an invitation for God's divine holiness to enter into our limited human experiences and efforts.

In part 1, we talked about the rhythm of our relationship with God, which begins with God and the incredible capacity he has placed in us and in creation. Here the pendulum swings back to us to consecrate who we are and what we have to him so that his presence, plan, and purposes enter our lives in a new and fresh way. In doing so, we are asking him to reorder our lives in a way that brings glory to him and life satisfaction to us.

Desperate for God

In business, we like to talk about "pivot points," the times when something—a project, trend, or stock price—meaningfully changes direction. People also have pivot points, like starting a new job, experiencing a death, meeting the person they'll someday marry, or even suffering a betrayal or loss. I can think of probably six or seven specific moments like this in my life that changed my ultimate trajectory and experience. Most of those events were brought about by a person, sometimes someone I didn't know well. But in the brief times our lives overlapped, something inside me changed.

One of those moments occurred when I was twenty-six years old. I was still working for that prestigious accounting firm, and they sent me on an assignment to Melbourne, Australia, for six months. This was before smartphones and wireless internet made it easy to stay connected, so as I sat on the airplane, traveling literally to the other side of the world, I felt overwhelmingly separated from everything and everyone I knew. I stared out the small airplane window, watching the curve of the earth, and thought there had to be more to life than I'd seen so far. *If I'm going to live seventy or eighty years and then be put in a grave*, I told myself, *I need to have more fun and not work as hard.*

But the Melbourne office had other ideas. They were determined to get their money's worth from me and loaded me with a number of client assignments. I worked long hours among strangers, then went home to my chilly apartment, which was heated by a small space heater that was more like a bright lightbulb than anything remotely warm. It was a lonely life for a young, single man.

And I was still living only for myself. Brueggemann describes a life that is absent of God as "one dimensional, flat, empty, and exhausted."[2] That sums up the way I felt. My focus was all about my pleasure, my work, my needs, and me. That kind of self-focus brought no happiness or satisfaction. It never does.

I met a young woman who was excited about a church called Richmond Temple. She couldn't stop talking about it, and what she described sounded nothing like what I remembered about the church I'd visited a few times at home in New England. Services there were long and boring, full of the pastor's stale jokes and strong opinions. Church, as I knew it, was nothing worth getting excited about.

But I was lonely and bored, so one day I decided to try this Australian church, Richmond Temple. The first thing I heard when I walked up was trumpet music, and the first thing I saw was a group of friendly people eager to shake my hand and welcome me. The service was nothing like what I expected. The music kept playing, and people were waving their hands in the air and praying out loud. The service lasted for hours.

To be honest, in that first visit, I was turned off by all the noise and forceful preaching of "the Word." When it was finally over, an elderly woman came over and handed me some pamphlets about the Bible. When I got back to my apartment, I threw the literature against a wall as hard as I could and said, "The day I need this will be a sad day."

But I was still lonely, and weekends stretched out, long and empty. I decided to go back to Richmond Temple under the premise that it was a sociological experiment. I would sit back, I decided, and observe Karl Marx's "opium of the masses" at work. I looked at these people—an international community of Greeks, Italians, and Australians—with all the smug confidence of youth and judged them as needy and naive.

Yet I kept attending. I didn't count on how the kind looks, welcoming words, invitations to dinners, and—most incredibly—visible answers to the prayers of these "simple" people would affect me. The congregation was mostly poor, and their prayers were full of both desperation and confidence. After months of hearing that Jesus is alive and is God's incarnate Son and the Bible is the Word of God, I had a strange thought.

What if this is true?

I was a cynical and, as I've shared, independent person. I'd also studied a healthy dose of statistics and math. While the kindness of strangers was melting my heart, I was unable to take the next step of faith. So the first prayer of my life went something like this: "Dear God, I have lived twenty-six years without hearing these things or meeting people like this. I've never seen you intervene in the world like you have here. How can this one sample of people in this one location be right and everyone else I've met in my life be wrong? If you can answer this question, I will give you everything. Amen."

Almost immediately, I heard a voice speak to my heart. "Jack, how many people have you known who really knew they needed me?"

From my detached, grieving family to my overachieving college friends and advisers to my work-hard, play-hard colleagues in corporate America, I realized for the first time I had always been surrounded by people who were independent and self-sufficient, or at least people who wanted to be those things. I didn't know anyone who admitted they needed anyone, let alone a Supreme Being.

I started to wonder, *What if the key to life is being desperate for God?*

I wanted to believe Jesus shed his blood to forgive everyone who believes and accepts his sacrifice as the atonement for their sins. I wanted to kneel at the cross. Yet I still argued with the people at Richmond Temple regarding the exclusiveness of the message.

At the end of the one Sunday morning was an altar call like no other I've ever heard. The pastor had preached about Jesus's encounter with the woman at the well and how Jesus promised her living water so that she would never thirst again. He invited anyone who was thirsty and needed forgiveness to come forward. He also said, "Do not come up if you are not willing to give Jesus everything you are and everything you have."

God tugged on my heart. I gulped. I knew I was like that woman; I needed the water Jesus was offering. But was I willing to give up everything? I didn't have much except my job and about $1,000 in the bank.

God kept tugging. Finally, I got up from the pew and went forward. I gave the church the money in my bank account and accepted Christ as my Lord and Savior.

My life has not been the same since that day.

Decades later, I recognize that what happened at that altar was not just my moment of salvation, although that's certainly true. God also called me, through the pastor's words, to do something else.

He called me to consecrate all that I was, all that I had, and all that I would ever be.

Finished Goods

As I studied this idea of consecration as a key to God's provision, my business mind kicked in and I started to see a pattern. The process and benefit of dedicating something to God, as Jesus did on the hillside, curiously overlapped with what I knew about, of all things, manufacturing.

Remember silica, the valuable element of sand I first described in chapter 1 that can be converted into microprocessors? To turn what's in your sandbox into the thing that makes your smartphone smart, manufacturers must first separate oxygen and other excess material from the silica. Then they put the silica in a furnace, scorching the sand to more than 2000 degrees Celsius. Doing so burns away the impurities, leaving only an ingot of pure silicon, which then can be processed into computer chips and other valuable material.

Silica isn't unique in this. To turn most raw materials, including crude oil, plants, and metals, into the products we use in our daily lives, scientists and manufacturers put them through an intense two-step process of *separation* and *purification*. This process actually changes the composition of the original material, turning it into something entirely different to be used in ways the original material could not.

Do you know crude oil is made from billions of dead microorganisms put under the right conditions for thousands of years? After it is extracted, the crude oil itself is separated, purified, and made into products such as auto fuel, lubricant, and chemical raw materials. Meanwhile, the pharmaceutical industry separates and purifies plants and chemicals into natural and synthetic drugs to meet health needs, and mines around the world separate and later purify metals.

Your daily life, from the cosmetics in your cabinet to the tires on your car, depends on the physical concept of consecration. Without separation and purification, we wouldn't be able to discover the capacity of creation's resources to become smartphones, gas, or plastic.

Our spiritual health relies on consecration as well. Without the separation that happened to me when I responded to the pastor in that Australian church and the purification that filled my life afterward, God couldn't have used me in the ways he has.

Separation and Purification

We are all flawed humans made up of raw materials that need to be separated and purified in order for us to experience the fullness of God's capacity and purposes for us.

We've talked already about the importance of a rhythm in our relationship with God as well as in his provision. As we act, he acts. We find this truth clearly played out in the act of consecration.

First, consecration involves a person setting something apart for God's glory and purposes to become holy. This must happen through deliberate decision and action.

God provides us with a model of this separation in John 10:36. Jesus was addressing the Jews in the temple courts who had asked if he was the Messiah. They had balked at his claim that all he had done had been authorized by the Father. He responded by describing himself as "the one whom the Father set apart as his very own and sent into the world."

God himself engaged in the process of setting apart his own Son, then Jesus carried the message forward to us in tangible ways we could witness.

On the hillside, by first acknowledging God and, we presume, inviting him to be part of the meal that was about to happen, Jesus *set apart* the five humble loaves of bread and two meager fish and dedicated them to being something much more than what they appeared to be.

Our lives, our gifts, and even our struggles can be consecrated when we invite God in and ask him to make them useful for his purposes. We'll explore more of what this looks like in the next chapter. For now, let's examine the second step of consecration.

Consecration is also about something God does. As we give him our offerings, he steps in and purifies them, making our offerings holy in a way we never could alone.

The key word here is *holy*. The holiness of God is what some theologians call "the otherness of God."[3] It is that which sets him apart from every other being. When we invite his "otherness" into our lives, it transforms whatever it touches in ways that are simply impossible apart from him.

We share some attributes with our Creator. He gave us some of his divine goodness, kindness, and love. He gave us free will and the ability to make our own decisions for or against him. It's our choice to invite him in, but only God can make something truly and completely holy.

"Who will not fear you, Lord, and bring glory to your name? For you alone are holy," writes the author of Revelation 15:4. In both Isaiah 6:3 and Revelation 4:8, the angels, the heavenly host, sing, "Holy, holy, holy," speaking to the transcendence of God and the qualities of the Trinity.

We cannot become holy through human will and effort. When God tells us to be holy, he is pointing us toward a process of separation and purification only he can bring about.

Our souls have contaminants (sin), and we require a purification process and his refining fire to be made acceptable.

The only way that happens is through consecration. The death of Christ on my behalf canceled out my moral indebtedness, serving as the ultimate purification. When I walked to the front of that church in Australia and willingly went into God's furnace, my spiritual impurities were stripped away, like the impurities from silica. The very composition of my soul changed. I was filled with God's holiness and became what the apostle Paul calls a "new creation" (2 Corinthians 5:17). I still fall short in many ways, but I was forgiven. I was loved. I was made into something new.

And now, with my new vision, I have the opportunity to extend the blessing of consecration, because this idea of inviting God's holiness extends past the one-time act of salvation.

Making All Things New

The idea of setting something aside—or sacrificing something—for God is not new. Take, for example, the Ten Commandments, where God told the Israelites to set aside the seventh day of the week, the Sabbath, as holy and different. He also told them to set apart their first sons, their best animals, and the firstfruits of their crops: "A tithe of everything from the land, whether grain from the soil or fruit from the trees, belongs to the LORD; it is holy to the LORD" (Leviticus 27:30).

Our modern understanding of this idea of a tithe is usually limited to an individual's financial resources, and then only to their annual income. But what the author of Leviticus shows us is that the potential of consecration is much wider. It is also much more influential than a mathematical equation. Our tithe is not an obligation; *it is an act of inviting holiness.*

As children of God, we can bring him anything and everything—our jobs, our children, our marriages, our gifts, our addictions and weaknesses, our time, our finances—to be used according to his purposes and open to his blessing. God can make every part of our lives holy if we invite him to do so. To live a life of consecration means living an ongoing, intentional message of "I am with you; let your holiness into everything I have been given."

Many years after that life-changing moment at Richmond Temple in Melbourne, I was working for a wealthy European investor who trusted me to manage several of his businesses and invest his money in new ventures. At one point, I was in the middle of a very complicated acquisition of a company in Atlanta for my employer. It was a risky endeavor, both for him and for me. So every Sunday a friend and I would meet and, in a time of heartfelt prayer, consecrate the transaction and whatever business came from it to the Lord. We asked that God would do something special with this small Atlanta company for his honor and glory.

The deal finally went through, and the business blossomed. My boss made his investment back a hundred times over. When I left the company fifteen years later, it had become the second-largest American firm in its industry, employing five thousand workers and providing stability for many families. That one small company had grown, as we had prayed, into something that would truly influence and impact the people of Atlanta for years to come.

And that's not an isolated story. Over and over, I've seen God bless the people, decisions, and opportunities I've consecrated to him. He desires to redeem not only the big things and the major moments but also the seemingly unimportant details.

If I ask God to consecrate a specific one-dollar bill and not a different one, does it really make a difference? Can a marriage, a child, or a business deal change when it is consecrated for God's glory and purposes? I have too many physical and practical examples that say *yes* for me to give you any other answer.

Jesus, seeing the need around him, invited God into the solution, and God provided. I believe that when Jesus prayed over the bread and the fish, their composition actually changed. They were filled with a new quality—a holiness—that allowed them to be multiplied.

While the physical composition of that dollar or that relationship may not change as it did with the bread and the fish, this is what I do think happens: when we reverently invite God's power, presence, and purposes into anything, something shifts in the heavenlies.

In his commentary on Matthew, theologian William Barclay makes an interesting point about the parable in Matthew 13:33, where Jesus compares the kingdom of God to leaven working through all the dough. According to Barclay, in Jewish language and thought, leaven is almost viewed with suspicion. The Jews rely on unleavened bread and food for their feasts and Passover celebrations. Barclay wonders, then, if Jesus chose this illustration of the kingdom deliberately. His disciples and the others who were listening would have felt a certain shock at hearing the kingdom of God compared to leaven; this certainly would have drawn their attention, as an unusual or unexpected illustration always does.

Barclay writes, "The whole point of the parable lies in one thing . . . the overwhelming power of the leaven. Leaven *changed* the character of a whole baking. The introduction of the leaven causes a *transformation* in the dough; and the coming of the Kingdom causes a transformation in life" (emphasis added).[4]

As a businessman who has worked for much of his career leading service companies, I have always told people that Jesus was in the service industry. After all, he said, "I am among you as one who serves" (Luke 22:27). But when we study consecration, we see that he is also in the manufacturing, mining, and health care businesses, because he also said, "I am making everything new!" (Revelation 21:5).

Pushing Holiness Aside

Despite the promises associated with consecration and even the outright instructions in Scripture to submit ourselves to God's separation and purification, too many people leave consecration out of their daily lives. They may have given their hearts to Jesus, but in this fractured, fragmented, scarcity-driven world, they aren't ready or don't think to give him the things that fill their everyday lives.

I believe that's because the modern world and its philosophies have been so deeply influenced by the opposite of holiness.

In 1776, while we were busy fighting for independence from England here in America, on the other side of the world, Scottish philosopher and economist Adam Smith was writing the classic text *The Wealth of Nations*. In it, Smith suggests that even as people pursue their own self-interests in the ways they seek to generate wealth, an unintentional good is created that benefits society at large. He famously refers to an "invisible hand" that seems to guide the process.

Smith did not intend for this invisible hand to be read as the hand of God. At the dawn of the Industrial Age, he was surrounded by steadily expanding wealth and influence. As Europe shifted away from feudal governments and continued to expand into new corners of the world, opportunities seemed limitless. The rising tides of manufacturing, exploration, and global trade expanded the middle class and provided paths of opportunity for people at all levels of the social and economic strata. If one entrepreneur established a trade route or built a factory, the expansion of jobs and resources created opportunities for many others.

Almost 250 years later, things have certainly changed. With the Enlightenment, individuals, communities, and entire governments began to eschew the idea that human life has some purpose, guided by a higher power. Untethered from a common morality or set of spiritual morals, ethics became a matter of individual preference. Simultaneously, the opportunities that had supported growing economies began to disappear.

I can't reasonably write a book about living in a time of fear and scarcity without addressing the questions of wealth inequality and the economic divisions that have left so many families feeling abandoned and abused over the past forty years.

One way to look at the changes is to blame technology and the ways it disproportionately benefits only a few. A hundred years ago, Henry Ford invented the Model T car, but he needed a factory full of workers to produce the cars. In 1914, he employed more than 13,000 workers to make

260,000 cars on his state-of-the-art assembly lines, paying them more than double the average manufacturing wage and significantly changing their quality of life, while still personally benefiting handsomely in the process.[5]

Compare that to WhatsApp, a clever global messaging technology created by a handful of entrepreneurs. In early 2014, creators bragged the app had reached 420 million users, served by only fifty-five employees. Facebook purchased the app that fall for $19 billion. That's more than the total wealth of entire countries—and it was given to just a few individuals.[6]

Something has happened fundamentally in our society. Where did these extreme profit margins, salaries, and wealth concentrations of our present economy come from? And what does this have to do with consecration?

As I look at history, I can only say that the challenges of inequality, and the stress and frustration that come from them, stem not from God's absence in our lives—because he is never absent—but from the secularization that now drives our culture.

Very simply, consecration is inviting God and his holiness into the details of our lives. Secularization, however, pushes God and his holiness out of our lives.

I recognize that secularization can be a loaded word in today's polarized society. I don't mean to use it in the way we commonly hear it used in political or media debates about the separation of church and state. That is part of the conversation, perhaps, but it doesn't go far enough.

Just as true consecration is much more than the theme of a Sunday morning service, secularization is more than the debate over whether there should be a Nativity scene in front of the city hall building at Christmas. Egyptian scholar Abdel

Wahab El-Messiri was the first to define the difference between the state-only idea of partial secularization and a complete secularization, which he called "the separation between all values . . . *so that the holiness is removed from the world,* and this world is transformed into a usable matter that can be employed *for the sake of the strong*" (emphasis added).[7]

The "set apart" faith of God's followers and the holiness of God's Spirit in the world are like the leaven Jesus described, working their way through every part of society. I am convinced that the growing gap between the rich and the poor that endangers our entire society is a direct result of this secularization process in which "holiness is removed from the world." It is the very presence and grace of God that compel us to bless . . . and lift others up! Secularization, in its broadest sense, removes that presence, power, and vitality—that holiness—from our actions, both corporately and individually. It denies the central role the Creator plays in the creation. In the void, we're left with an anxiety-filled society marked by inequality and strife. If humans, as God's creations, are not reflecting his divine attributes of compassion, concern, and respect for others, then there's nothing to hold us back from indulging in a scarcity mind-set.

Even analysts at Goldman Sachs, the lion of the free market economy, looked at the current state of the world and concluded in a 2016 report that if "wrong and high" corporate profit margins continue, "there are broader questions to be asked about the efficacy of capitalism."[8] Both a leading investment firm and an Egyptian scholar are pointing to destructive outcomes that I believe stem from this process of secularization.

I look at the world as it is today and am convinced that when God is sidelined, there is no check to human ambition, and the inequalities widen. Secularization in this context is the opposite of consecration, driven by the human quest for control and to become our own gods. This is the spiritual war we now find ourselves in. Only inviting the true invisible hand back into the public space will restore order.

Consecration is important because it invites God's holiness in. When we ignore the value of God's holiness and push him out of the way and try to purify things on our own, we fail. People get hurt. The sense of scarcity that fills the world now, the feeling that there is not enough, is present because we alone are not enough. Only God is enough.

Unlocking God's provision begins with reversing the secularization process and learning to invite him, the One who provides, into the details of our lives. When we invite God's holiness in and acknowledge our dependence on him to change and purify what we can't, he changes us and our surroundings. He brings provision to our actions.

God's Rhythm of Provision for You: Consecration

The first section on capacity revealed that God created more in us, others, and his creation than we had imagined. We asked him for eyes to see and believe, for him to open doors, and for power over capacity killers.

In this second step of unlocking God's provision, we invite his presence, power, and holiness into our strengths, weaknesses, and circumstances.

In John 15:5, Jesus says, "Apart from me you can do nothing." We need to understand that God often provides after he is invited in and asked to reorder things.

Say a short prayer and ask him to come into your life in a new way and reorder it for his glory. Ask him for strength through Christ and to forgive you for your sins.

In the area of consecration, evaluate yourself on a scale of 1 to 10:

1 I am struggling with this idea of "inviting him in."

5 I am willing to give consecration a shot but have real doubts.

10 I prayed and asked God to do a new thing in a number of areas in my life. I am anxious to see what he will do.

Your score: _____

Enter your score on page 211.

4

An Acceptable Sacrifice

The Path of Consecration

Bobby Richardson played second base for the New York Yankees from 1955 to 1966. An outspoken Christian, he went on to be a motivational speaker who devoted a great deal of time and energy to the Fellowship of Christian Athletes (FCA). At one FCA event, Richardson opened with an eleven-word prayer: "Dear God, your will. Nothing more, nothing less, nothing else. Amen."

That's what it means to be consecrated to God and his kingdom. We yield everything to him—every fiber of our being, every moment of our time, every possession in our care. We make *his* will *our* will.

Nothing more, nothing less, nothing else.

"Consecrate yourselves," Joshua told the Israelites just before he led them across the Jordan River and into the land promised to them, "for tomorrow the LORD will do amazing things among you" (Joshua 3:5). And God did, indeed, do amazing things. The people prayed, and the very next morning God stopped the Jordan, swollen and deep in its flood stage, giving them a dry and safe place to pass into their new homeland.

It's easy to get excited about a promise like that and to eagerly pray for our own miracles, but consecration isn't as simple as one prayer = one miracle. Consecration asks a great deal from us. Perhaps that is why, in the back and forth of our rhythmic relationship with God, consecration is an aspect we often misunderstand.

Like Jesus's disciples looking out over the crowd on the hillside, we get distracted by the overwhelming need we're facing and forget about the powerful support standing right beside us. Even after we experience salvation's emotional release or witness God working in the lives of people around us, we are not convinced of his daily involvement with us directly. Perhaps we don't feel worthy. Maybe, because of our limited human perspective, we just can't grasp the possibility of a miracle. We want to believe Jesus will care for and provide for us, but something holds us back. So we continue to clutch whatever control we have over whatever gifts we've been given. We continue to be stuck in that place that is the opposite of holiness—one dimensional, flat, empty, and exhausted. We fail to see how to separate ourselves and prepare for his holiness to change us.

The Gift of Everything

If most people think of consecration at all, it's in the context of their finances. After all, money is the cornerstone of how the world interacts. It is also, from a spiritual perspective, usually considered dangerous. Jesus labeled money as "unrighteous," the "mammon" that draws our attention and our loyalty away (Luke 16:9 NKJV).

After more than thirty years working in business, I have no problem talking about money. It's what I know.

But I want to be very clear that the heart of consecration is not tied to some preset number of dollars or hours. God's blessing does not flow down onto us because we check the right boxes of behavior. Instead, God and money are really about worship and sacrifice.

Most churches today don't try to connect the ideas of worship and sacrifice. We think of worship as what happens when we sing, and sacrifice as what happens when we pass the offering plate. However, the Bible explains things differently. One of the first instances of worship in the Bible appears in Genesis 22, when Abraham is told to sacrifice his precious son Isaac on Mt. Moriah. After they walk far into the wilderness, Abraham stops and tells his servants to "stay here with the donkey while I and the boy go over there. We will worship and then we will come back to you" (v. 5).

Abraham planned to worship God by sacrificing to him the son he loved more than anything.

Pastor Crawford Loritts of Fellowship Bible Church says, "Every sacrifice is an investment."[1] When we are willing to give God what is most valuable to us, we are not letting it go forever. We are entrusting it to the One who will protect and imbue it with life.

Consecration isn't about giving 10 percent of our income to a church or ministry. It's about a change of perspective, offering *everything* God gave us back to him. After all, if you are a parent, do you care only about how your child handles his or her allowance? Or do you also care about whether your children treats his or her siblings and friends well? Wouldn't you be prouder if your child was recognized for citizenship or service to the community? So it's not a stretch to realize that God cares about what we do with all the things in our lives: our time, creativity, relationships, gifts, commitment to the needy, and capacity.

He wants us to give him our jobs, our money, and our relationships. He wants to be part of the decisions about where we live and how we spend our time.

Our human, scarcity-driven nature wants to store up what is ours and set it aside for a rainy day. God asks that instead we give him everything and then trust him to do what's best. He will do something special to our sacrifices, but it's not always what we expect. Sometimes he consumes the sacrifice, knowing we are better off without it. Other sacrifices he gives back to us, instilled with his power and purposes with capacity far beyond what we could bring on our own.

As with the miracle of the loaves and fish, what God can do goes beyond what we can see and into a whole different dimension of experience.

That kind of radical change carries enormous risk, of course. God called Abraham to give him the most important thing in his life, the son he'd waited a hundred years for, with no guarantee that his boy would be returned. Abraham could only trust in the "other" that belongs to God alone—his holiness.

I can relate to Abraham's experience. As with Abraham, the most important things Lisa and I have are our sons. Years ago, when they were still young, I remember reading Psalm

127:4, which says, "Like arrows in the hands of a warrior are children born in one's youth." It changed my perspective to realize that my most valuable treasure could be used as an offensive weapon! As our sons grew, we held on to that verse as we allowed them to enter challenging situations, whether it was attending a high school that did not share our values and beliefs or going on a mission trip to Bosnia during the war there. Perhaps the most difficult moment came when our youngest son shared his desire to become a Black Hawk helicopter pilot. We prayed long and hard over that desire, consecrating him and his subsequent service in Iraq to God. And in each case, we saw God move in their lives, providing friendships and doors of blessing and provision.

What would come to mind if I were to ask you, What is the most important thing in your life? Everyone's treasure is different, but I've never met a person who didn't have something they would rather shelter and protect than put at risk by giving it over to God. Yet often those are the very things God most wants us to entrust to him.

Where Do You Put Your Faith?

As Christians, we are aware of specific things that are simply part of the faith. Most of us know the Bible calls us to tithe. We also probably know we *should* volunteer our time at a food bank or at our church. And one Sunday when our children are small, we dress them up and bring them to church because tradition dictates we *should* christen or dedicate them.

We act in obedience, but sometimes we are just hedging our bets against the things we know we can't control. We check the boxes of what God "expects" and think, *Surely that's enough. In these uncertain times, God can't ask for more than that.* So we go back to our regular lives, with all the day-to-day stresses and unanswered questions about the future. We put our faith in what we can see—our bank accounts, our work ethic, our government, our families. We push aside the needs of others, thinking government services, disaster relief funds, and other people will solve those problems. We have too much on our plates already as we try to control everything around us, worrying about the future.

Like the disciples, we doubt what we cannot see. We fear what we cannot control.

And that's just the way the enemy wants it. In the spiritual war that rages around us, fear is one of Satan's greatest weapons. He uses fearful thinking to drive unbelief, creating a wedge between our human interpretations and God's divine and holy provision. He dissuades us from sacrifice, whispering that God doesn't really care about our day-to-day lives. He blocks us from receiving the fullness of God's blessing by focusing our attention on other things—on idols.

One of my favorite verses is Jonah 2:8–9: "Those who cling to worthless idols turn away from God's love for them. But I, with shouts of grateful praise, will sacrifice to you. What I have vowed I will make good."

This was a hard-learned lesson for the prophet Jonah, whom my mother used to quiz me about many years ago. God had called him to preach to the Assyrian people of Nineveh, longtime enemies of the Israelites. Jonah didn't want to go. He tried to run away instead, jumping on a boat that was going anywhere except to the place where God had called him. But God sent a storm that tossed the boat and threatened the lives of everyone on board. Knowing this was his punishment, Jonah told the sailors to throw him overboard to save their own lives. They did, and a "huge fish" swallowed Jonah, saving his life but putting him in an uncomfortable position. After three days of surviving inside the fish, Jonah came to his senses and called out to the Lord for help.

When we put anything ahead of God in our hearts—even our own safety, as Jonah did—we turn our backs on God's love and forfeit our place in his provision. Imagine choosing to forfeit "amazing grace" to cling to a false god. By surrendering these idols, we open up space in our lives to receive God's mercy and grace.

Idols are the things we feel are too important to give to God. They are, even when we know better than to use the words, the things that are more important to us than God.

The enemy knows our weak spots. He knows we want to protect our children, to provide for our families, to not be a burden. He tells us our first priority must be our own comfort and security, especially in indigent and uncertain times. Satan preys on our fears and convinces us we must rely on ourselves to secure our situation.

The tentacles of disbelief slide into our faith, weakening it, and we start to trust our bank accounts more than the One who gave them to us. Will a consecrated dollar or person or decision really be different from one that's not consecrated?

I want to be clear: money, in itself, is not wrong. It is a necessary and useful commodity to keep the practical systems running smoothly. Moreover, wealth in and of itself is not condemned in the Bible. Several figures in the Old and New Testaments are noted, without negative judgment, as being wealthy: Abraham, Jacob, Job, King David, Joseph of Arimathea, Philemon, and Aquila and Priscilla.

However, making money into an idol and turning to it instead of to God leads us into Satan's trap and away from God's best plan for us. God—not money—is our provider. Often the test as to whether money has become an idol is the extent to which we are willing to risk it for God's kingdom.

We can rely on God or money but not on both. At times, you may feel you have everything under control, that you are being a wise steward of your resources. But if the economy has taught us anything in the past decade, it's that we can rely on nothing on this earth. In Proverbs 23:5, we're told that riches can "sprout wings and fly off to the sky like an eagle." Jeremiah 48 and 49 warn of the downfall of various nations due to the ways they trusted in and boasted of their riches, being arrogant in their wealth. Our houses—or at least the value of our houses—might crumble. The savings we tucked away in the bank, counting on them to be safe for the future, can be taken from us. Human promises of provision might be rescinded.

The idol of money is a counterfeit source of provision and safety. It seems to meet our needs for a season, but in the end—whether we have a million dollars or a pile of debt—it will enslave us and leave us desperate.

Only God will never fail. Only he can be trusted to protect and use what is his.

Everything we have is his.

False Prophets

Money isn't the only idol that keeps us from the experience of consecrating all our gifts and resources to God.

Anyone who draws our attention away from God or anything we dedicate ourselves or our resources to instead of God is an idol. At times, idols are clearly unworthy or evil things. At other times, they manifest themselves as good things that supplant God's best. They draw our attention away from eternal matters, encouraging us to trust our bodies, our wardrobes, and our 401(k)s. They shove headlines in our faces and whisper dire warnings in our ears.

Perhaps no human idol is as insidious and as dangerous to the true kingdom of God as the false prophet who pretends to be God's mouthpiece while corrupting the Father's message.

You've seen these false prophets on television or streaming online—or perhaps you've read the headlines about recent government and media investigations into their "ministries." They are the self-proclaimed "evangelists" and "ministers" who spend most of their time encouraging their audiences to trust their money to a specific ministry rather than to God. They shamelessly claim their right to private jets and luxury mansions as rewards for their "faithfulness" to God and promise that their followers are entitled to this kind of lavish living as well, but only if they are willing to put a check in the mail.

These false teachers reassure the most vulnerable and desperate people among us that it is God's job to please them and meet their needs and that it is their responsibility to support the ministers who live enviable lives of prosperity.

I've seen churches employ high-pressure sales tactics to prey on those who are desperate for a miracle and those who can least afford the heretical promises. They take Jesus's parable of the seeds and corrupt it by claiming that *they* are the fertile soil. They deny the open promises and risk of what true consecration means and instead demand only dedication to themselves and their own empty promises.

Is there any clearer example of a human idol? Is there anyone who does more damage to the true message of God's provision?

Economists use the term *moral hazard* to describe a situation in which a party gets involved in a risky event believing there will be no consequences if they fail; they are protected against the risk, because the other party will have to incur the cost. The secular world has seen plenty of examples of moral hazards in the last few years. Banks and financial firms pushed our economy over a cliff in the subprime mortgage crisis. Loan originators, appraisers, real estate agents, credit advisory firms, and Wall Street firms all participated in what is now considered massive fraud. Yet practically speaking, there were few long-term consequences for the "too big to fail" businesses. The Federal Reserve System allowed firms to borrow money at 0 percent interest and restore their balance sheets. Meanwhile, families were left bankrupt, their homes foreclosed and their credit destroyed. The failure associated with risk was borne by another party.

Plenty of televangelists play the moral hazard card as well. They put forward a promise of prosperity, making grand promises that ignore our own responsibility and risk within the relationship. They demand that their followers—the other party—sacrifice deeply. But when they seek only their own desires, and not the will of the Lord, there's no blessing. When the oil packets and prayer cloths don't work, and it becomes clear that God doesn't hand out material blessings on demand, the only party that incurs a cost is the one who trusted the false prophet.

God's true provision doesn't benefit one believer over another. God's plan hinges on his own willingness to bear our sins and brokenness. In Wall Street terms, he is the "counterparty" who shoulders our burdens in perpetuity.

Pleasing Sacrifices

God offers us provision, blessing, and the opportunity to live within his limitless capacity. What does he expect in return?

The ultimate form of consecration comes when we give over our very selves, our lives, to God. Paul discusses this in Romans 12:1: "Therefore, I urge you, brothers and sisters, in view of God's mercy, to offer your bodies as a living sacrifice, holy and pleasing to God—this is your true and proper worship."

Consecration is about sacrifice. The Old Testament is full of rules about what to sacrifice and how to make sacrifices, covering everything from cooking pots to animals, and there were many ways to sacrifice incorrectly.

The Bible offers several stories of acceptable and unacceptable sacrifices, beginning with the first humans born on earth, Abel and Cain.

> In the course of time Cain brought some of the fruits of the soil as an offering to the LORD. And Abel also brought an offering—fat portions from some of the firstborn of his flock. The LORD looked with favor on Abel and his offering, but on Cain and his offering he did not look with favor. So Cain was very angry, and his face was downcast. (Gen. 4:3–5)

Bible scholars disagree over why Cain's sacrifice was unacceptable. Some say it was because Abel's was a blood sacrifice, while Cain's was not. Others point out that Scripture says Abel specifically brought firstfruits, while Cain may not have. Still others say the problem lay in Cain's attitude, not in the nature of his offering. I don't presume to interpret the story beyond what God gave us, but I can draw a conclusion: we should endeavor to give God our first and our best with an attitude that honors him.

Let's look at Exodus 28, which is an entire chapter dedicated to the very specific guidelines for consecrating Aaron, Moses's brother and the first high priest of the chosen people, through the particular clothing he would wear before the Lord. The chapter begins:

> Make sacred garments for your brother Aaron to give him dignity and honor. Tell all the skilled workers to whom I have given wisdom in such matters that they are to make garments for Aaron, for his consecration, so he may serve me as priest. (vv. 2–3)

God then outlines everything from the turban on Aaron's head to the undergarments he and his descendants must wear under their clothes "so that they will not incur guilt and die" (v. 43). God's priests could not wear whatever they wanted. They could not stroll blithely into the Holy of Holies in a T-shirt and shorts. In their obedience and careful preparation to meet their Creator, the Israelite priests acknowledged that they were not their own; they belonged to God and were set apart for him. They acted out their consecration by engaging in particular rituals. With this consecration came certain appropriate boundaries. There were right ways and wrong ways to be priests, and God made the rules.

This idea of boundaries and expectations is a struggle for many people. We live in a society that resists calling anything "unacceptable." We reward effort as well as outcome, and we hand out participation medals. How dare someone, even God, say my best isn't good enough, that there are standards for me to live up to.

The difficult truth is that good intentions are not always enough.

I was reminded of this a few years ago when a friend invited me to join him for a round of golf on Long Island at a famous course called Shinnecock Hills. My friend was not a member of this very exclusive, very expensive club, but he knew a member who had offered to be our sponsor for the day. We could use this member's name to set up a tee time, even if he wasn't present.

It was a once-in-a-lifetime kind of opportunity, and my friend and I arrived early, excited to be there. We hit a few balls on the practice greens, bought things in the pro shop, and had a delicious lunch in the club dining room. But when we showed up at the first tee and my friend confidently named our sponsor, we were told that no such person was a member there. Suddenly, it was obvious we were interlopers instead of welcome guests, and we were politely asked to leave the grounds.

It turned out my friend had confused two clubs, and we actually had a tee time at a different club right down the road. How embarrassing!

We had the right intentions, and we had the clubs to play golf, but we were still not allowed to play at Shinnecock. We had not been "set apart" by a Shinnecock member.

What's important to remember is that our sacrifices must be holy—and that happens after consecration. God sees the motives in our hearts as well as our actions. He has given us a way to be absolutely righteous and forgiven through the shed blood of Jesus. When we stand on his merit, not our own, our will is his will and our best is more than enough.

First Timothy 4:4–5 says, "For everything God created is good, and nothing is to be rejected if it is received with thanksgiving, because it is consecrated by the word of God and prayer."

It doesn't matter whether we can offer God a banquet full of food or a few small fish. It's the attitude with which we present our offering that matters. Every sacrifice is an investment, and an acceptable sacrifice is a good seed planted that will bear fruit. The more things we consecrate, the more yield there will be.

That yield will result in provision for us, others, and the kingdom in general.

To make a pleasing sacrifice and an acceptable consecration, we must begin by acknowledging God as the true center of our lives. Our love for him will determine what we are willing to lay at his feet in worship.

A Seed of Faith

For years, I thought sanctification was something God did to me. It was a one-sided experience that would happen throughout the rest of my life.

But that's not the way relationships work. Of course God can do whatever he wants, but he's never tried to force a relationship on people he created in love. He doesn't beat down the door and push his way into our lives or our decisions. Instead, he patiently and constantly waits for us to take the next step to deepening the relationship, pursuing and wooing us to a place of surrender. He remains, blessings in hand, until we invite him into each specific corner of our lives.

When my sons were younger, we used to watch those phony wrestling matches on TV together. In certain matches, the wrestlers had partners. If a wrestler was in trouble, about to get pinned or injured, he could touch the hand of his partner outside the ring. The partner would then jump in and take care of the opponent.

In the same way, a prayer of consecration invites the Holy One to come in and take over with the capacity only he can offer. Through this prayer, we acknowledge our need for separation and purification.

"Idols cannot simply be removed," says Tim Keller. "They must be replaced. If you only try to uproot them, they grow back, but they can be supplanted. By what? By God himself, of course. But by God we do not mean a general belief in his existence. Most people have that, yet their souls are riddled with idols. What we need is a living encounter with God."[2]

Consecration means identifying the idols that keep us from giving everything to God, whether they are our jobs, children, marriages, bank accounts, or false prophets. It means letting go of those idols and believing God will step in to replace them and fill us in ways they never could. At the same time, it means holding on to that small grain of faith, the seed that, when planted, will grow into whatever God wants it to be.

Specific, significant moments in life—baptisms, communions, weddings, and even funerals—are natural places for us to pause, consider the gifts and opportunities before us, and choose to give them back to the Creator who first gave them to us.

Lisa and I got on our knees on our wedding night and committed any children that God might give us, before they were even conceived, back to him. I wanted our children to be offensive weapons to be used for his kingdom and his benefit, and they have been. As years passed, I was tempted on more than one occasion to question God or to say, "Lord, as a father, I would never subject my child to that." But my children are not mine; they never have been. And so I will lay them on the altar of worship time after time and trust God to do what he sees best.

But consecration isn't just for the big moments of life. In the Old Testament, the Israelites consecrated animals, utensils, and a host of everyday things to the Lord.

I've told you already about how I regularly consecrate my business and work life to God's glory. I do the same with the profits and bonuses that come from my investments. If I put two hundred dollars into a project and it comes back tenfold, that money is not mine. It is God's, and it is up to him to show me where he wants it spent. Sometimes he wants me to meet the need of someone in our community. Sometimes he wants me to support a ministry. And sometimes he wants to bless my family. But whatever the answer is, I am always only the humble conduit. The increase always belongs to the Lord.

If you ask, "Lord, what is your purpose and plan? How can this be used for your glory?" God will direct you. He can use anything, even what seems like the most trivial encounter or chore, if you give it to him.

Praying this way is not easy, and it won't always bring the answer we think we want—let alone the riches the false prophets promise. Romans 8:28 reminds us that "in all things God works for the good of those who love him, who have been called according to his purpose," but it doesn't say all things will make us happy, rich, or even healthy. This type of prayer is difficult, because it takes away some of our control and calls on God to work out his purposes with our assets, our habits, and even our liabilities.

Separation and sacrifice are linked together. God intended for the love relationship between us to be undergirded by our acts of giving him our first and best. That includes our time, money, children, and possessions. He knew this would test our love, but he intended it for our good, knowing that anything we would not set apart for him would become an idol and might ultimately destroy us.

As one of my former pastors liked to say, "Being in the will of God is the second most dangerous place to be." So set yourself apart for God's purposes and invite his holiness and truth to guide every step of your life. Then watch what he does and see how he provides.

God's Rhythm of Provision for You: Sacrifice

God doesn't want just your money or your time; he wants all of you! But our hearts are inclined to make idols out of the things and people in our lives that compete for God's place in our hearts.

According to Jonah 2:8, "Those who cling to worthless idols turn away from God's love for them." Is it sometimes scary to consecrate the people and things that mean the most to you? Absolutely! But think of the grace that could be yours. It helps to realize that every sacrifice is an investment on which God *will* give you a return.

Think about the people and circumstances in your life. Identify your idols and ask God to replace them. Ask God in prayer, "Lord, what is your purpose and plan? How can this be used for your glory?"

In the area of sacrifice, evaluate yourself on a scale of 1 to 10:

1 I do not understand or see the need to give or sacrifice things to God, especially the most important people and things.

5 I am willing to take a small step here and meet a need of someone or make a small financial gift.

10 I understand that sacrifices are investments and that they show God and people how much we love them. I have prayed and my heart is open to give generously of myself to God and others.

Your score: _____

Enter your score on page 211.

Part 3

CHALLENGES

Taking the five loaves and the two fish and looking up to heaven, he gave thanks *and broke them.* Then he gave them to the disciples to distribute to the people.

Luke 9:16, emphasis added

5

The Wilderness and the Marketplace

When God Brings Challenges

In June 2014, I stood on a hill in southern Israel looking out over the Judean wilderness. The view was breathtaking; barren, desolate hills, devoid of vegetation, stretched as far as I could see. It was beautiful, but nothing like what I had expected. Was this the "good and spacious land, a land flowing with milk and honey" that God promised to Moses (Exodus 3:8)? I had expected a forest and instead found total emptiness.

Our guide, Charlie Dyer, recognized my surprise and reminded me of another description of the Promised Land: "The land you are entering to take over is not like the land of Egypt, from which you have come, where you planted your seed and irrigated it by foot as in a vegetable garden. But the land you are crossing the Jordan to take possession of is a land of mountains and valleys that drinks rain from heaven. It is a land the LORD your God cares for" (Deuteronomy 11:10–12).

Charlie explained that the Judean land was particularly arid, with no natural bodies of water. Living things there were dependent on a few underground springs and, as Moses said, rain from heaven. I thought about how the Israelites were coming from the fertile valley that surrounded the Nile River, which was as much as a third of a mile wide in places. The rich soil fed by the Nile made growing crops easy. It took just a nudge of the foot, according to Moses; people didn't even need to bend over to irrigate their land! And now here they were, in the middle of a desert. Their sheep and goats could graze in the vast open spaces and produce milk, and the meadows could provide flowers for honey, but it would not be an easy existence. The people could prosper here, but they would have to depend on God's provision to survive.

They were in the wilderness, and they didn't always like it. Even though they'd been rescued from dangerous, back-breaking slavery, time after time the Israelites complained that they wished they were back in Egypt.

Humans generally dislike the wilderness, whether we're talking about the literal plains of Israel or the metaphorical season we all experience at one time or another, the one Dr. Bill Lawrence, in his book *Wilderness Wanderings*, describes as "those arid, barren patches of life—whether spiritual, physical, or emotional—that God takes us to in order to test us, transform us, purify us, prove us, and prepare us for His greatness in our lives."[1]

The wilderness is where life gets hard, relationships get messy, and challenges test our faith and stamina. It's a place where fear can grow. But the wilderness is also a place where

God and his abundance reside. It is where God takes what is broken, messy, or difficult and shows us how to reorder it for his glory and, often, for our own satisfaction and provision. But the wilderness is never easy. In the previous sections, we beheld in wonder the capacity that God created in us, others, and creation. We learned what it means to invite him into our lives, to let him reorder and provide. These changes can be stressful and sometimes even heartbreaking.

Understanding how to approach the challenges of our own wilderness experiences is the third aspect of our rhythmic relationship with God. The wilderness is another way God shows his provision for us. It is also where the battle for our souls becomes most intense. Here we face our biggest challenge: to realize that God is good and that his plan is not only for us but also often for the benefit of many others. Our future provision will come through these new people and new circumstances that he ushers into our lives.

When Jesus broke the loaves and fish, he showed us something about the wilderness. Before the bread could multiply into a blessing for everyone nearby, it first had to be torn to pieces.

This is a hard lesson to learn. We want a giant river to feed our crops. We want the big, red "Easy" button that the commercials for the national office supply store promise. We want things to work smoothly.

Christians tend to speak of the metaphorical desert or wilderness in hushed, almost apologetic tones. "Well, God seems to have you in the wilderness right now," says the well-meaning person when they hear about a difficult season of parenting or a loss or a stressful career or challenging family season. "Hang in there. You will get through it."

They make these difficult seasons sound like a trip to the spiritual dentist—something to get through as quickly as possible.

For years, I thought of the wilderness in the same way. At best, challenges and loss were in my life to instill discipline, and, at worst, they served as a test or punishment. Would I remain faithful to my God and my beliefs? Was this happening because I had strayed too far from him?

I've told you my father died when I was nine years old. I found out about it on a chilly October morning when I awoke to the sound of screaming. Frightened and still rubbing the sleep from my eyes, I ran down the hall to my parents' bedroom and found my mother and two older sisters wailing in absolute despair.

For me, my father's death came suddenly. Only later did I learn that he knew he had leukemia for at least a year, but he and my mother chose not to tell my sisters or me. There were no good-byes or wishes for good luck. There were no words of counsel or blessing. He was just gone.

My mother practiced Christian Science, a metaphysical belief system that, in my view, is neither Christian nor science. Its church claims that sickness is an illusion that can be corrected by prayer and the right way of thinking. My mother believed my father would get well if they controlled how they thought about his illness. She saw his death as a sign of her failure of faith. The minister who came to our house later that day supported this false belief and offered no words of comfort. "Today," he said to me, "the will of God was frustrated by the death of your father."

Whatever mental picture I had of God collapsed at that moment. Growing up, I'd heard that God is love, that God is all-powerful. But if God's will could be "frustrated" by death, I thought, then what was the use? I couldn't count on a God like that.

That was my attitude until I finally met my Savior, who was both loving and all-powerful, in that Melbourne church. Excited that God was now my eternal Father, I believed I would be immune to the wilderness since I was now "right" with God. He loved me, so he would protect me from any real hardship.

That false belief lasted until just before I left Australia, when a man from the church said he wanted to share a verse of Scripture with me. He wrote the reference on a slip of paper: Philippians 3:10.

"The apostle Paul wrote this," he told me. "'I want to know Christ—yes, to know the power of his resurrection and participation in his sufferings, becoming like him in his death.'"

I wasn't sure I liked the sound of that, especially the parts about "participation in his sufferings" and "like him in his death." I asked what it meant.

"Jack," he answered, "now that you're a Christian, God is going to use suffering in your life to change you and to make you more like him."

A few years passed, and I met and married Lisa. I was so excited to build a new family founded on genuine faith, and I dreamed about the blessings that would fill our life together. Instead, the wilderness descended on the first decade of our marriage with a vengeance.

Just a few months before our wedding, in an extremely rare circumstance, Lisa's sister Lauri contracted polio from her infant son's vaccination. She became a quadriplegic, unable to care for herself. And then to add insult to injury, her husband abandoned her and their son.

Then our home was robbed three times, leaving Lisa and me in a state of fear and loss. The third time there was nothing left to take but my clothes, and so the thieves emptied my dresser drawers.

Tragedy continued to strike when Lisa's mother suffered a heart attack. Her father was diagnosed with liver cancer and died less than nine months later. Another of Lisa's sisters was killed in a traffic accident, and her younger sister, still a teenager, became pregnant and gave the baby up for adoption.

I made myself sound confident when I told Lisa's sister Lauri I would manage her finances. I promised her, "You will never have to worry. Lisa and I will be there for you." But it was a statement of sheer faith in God's capacity, because I had very little confidence in my own financial wherewithal.

The family I had been excited to join became our dependents. Our finances were stretched impossibly thin. It felt as if a series of bombs had fallen, and the sense of burden was overwhelming.

Still grieving her family's losses, Lisa suffered through three difficult pregnancies in five years. Each was followed by a severe bout of postpartum depression that led to several hospital stays and lingering emotional challenges that followed her for years. My boys and I would pray for her every night. They would ask me, "Is Jesus going to make Mommy better?" And all I could say was, "Jesus is in control. He'll do the best thing for Mommy."

I began having a harder and harder time praying. Like many before me, I struggled to understand why my heavenly

Father would allow such things to happen to my family and me. I could not reconcile a God who loved me with a God who would allow me, and especially my dear wife, to go through such distress. My faith in God's character was under attack and badly shaken.

I was back in the wilderness, and I hated it.

Battles in the Wilderness

When Jesus was about thirty years old, he must have known his traveling ministry—the path that would eventually lead to his death—was about to begin. But first, the Bible says, he "was led by the Spirit into the wilderness" (Matthew 4:1; Luke 4:1).

We can assume the place he went was barren and empty. There was no village where he could buy supplies and no other people with whom to share his burden. I imagine the Mediterranean sun beating down on him as he fasted and prayed for forty days. At that point, Satan showed up, and the first thing he did was tempt Jesus to provide for *himself*.

"If you are the Son of God, tell these stones to become bread" (Matthew 4:3).

Satan's battle lines were drawn: a loving, just, and good God would not let us suffer. If the Son of God *could* provide, he *would*. But if this man in the wilderness couldn't provide for himself, Satan tried to conclude, then he was somehow weak or incapable.

Jesus, of course, knew better. He understood the appropriate context of God's provision. "Man shall not live on bread alone, but on every word that comes from the mouth of God," he reminded Satan (Matthew 4:4). But the tempter did not give up. He continued to test Jesus in every human weak point he could find.

Today the devil is still lurking in the wilderness, waiting to pounce on our moments of weakness. This is his ultimate battleground, the place he can find us where we are our most vulnerable and spread the lie that God doesn't care. The enemy of our souls wants to convince us that God's resources are limited and that his promises are undependable. He wants us to believe we live in scarcity, not abundance.

He isolates us and stokes the fires of our fears, telling us that the burden of our provision is our responsibility, not the responsibility of the One who promised to be our guide and give us our daily bread. Satan says we are alone and unloved. When things are bleak, he tells us we are failing and that God is failing too. If God cared, why would we be in this place? Why would we have to face cancer or theft or betrayal or loss? Why would God allow any of this to happen?

Those are questions we all ask at one time or another, but God alone has the answers.

Hebrews 11 has been called the Hall of Fame of Faith. It tells story after story of God's servants who lived in deep relationship with and total commitment to God, often in the face of terrible adversity and suffering. After reminding us of Old Testament heroes such as Noah, Abraham, Jacob, Joseph, and Moses, the writer then acknowledges the host of unnamed prophets who endured poverty, hunger, flogging, torture, imprisonment, death by torture, and on and on.

These were powerful verses for me when I was going through my own difficult times. While I've heard plenty of sermons about this chapter, I've rarely heard a minister or

Bible teacher call attention to one phrase in verse 34. It has become one of the most precious passages to me in all of God's Word. The author specifically acknowledges those "whose weakness was turned to strength."

Let's look at that same phrase in other translations. The King James Version says, "Out of weakness [they] were made strong." And the J. B. Phillips New Testament says, "From being weaklings they became strong men and mighty warriors."

These are powerful and reassuring statements for anyone who has ever gone through a time of suffering and weakness. The apostle Paul describes the same principle in 2 Corinthians 12:9–10 when he writes:

> But he [God] said to me, "My grace is sufficient for you, for my power is made perfect in weakness." Therefore I will boast all the more gladly about my weaknesses, so that Christ's power may rest on me. That is why, for Christ's sake, I delight in weaknesses, in insults, in hardships, in persecutions, in difficulties. For when I am weak, then I am strong.

Do we really believe that? Do we believe that, through the battles fought in the wilderness, God transforms our weaknesses into strength? Do we delight in our weaknesses and hardships, knowing that "when we are weak, then we are strong"? I am convinced this is a facet of God's abundance in our lives that we need to face and embrace.

God seemed to break my family. Yes, I had told God in Australia that I always wanted to desperately need him. But wasn't there an easier way? I found part of the answer in my relationship to the marketplace.

The Marketplace

As I've said, I hated the wilderness. It was barren, cold, and lonely. For me, and for many others, another place felt more like home. I call it the marketplace.

Perhaps because of the insecurity of my childhood, I was always drawn to numbers. I felt safe in the space I found to be rational and predictable, guided by the rules of economics and capitalism. The ideas of business and commerce made sense to me as an accountant and then as an executive. Capital was allocated efficiently. Goods and services were produced according to economies of scale. Prices were made honest through competition, and jobs developed workers and improved society. Shareholders received a return for the risks they took. I looked at the commercial world humans had developed and relied on for centuries and saw that my basic needs for shelter, food, and sanitation could efficiently be met.

In the marketplace, I could see the invisible hand guiding the exchange of products and ideas. This was my land of milk and honey, both of which I could easily locate on grocery store shelves. In fact, there were multiple brands of each to suit my personal preference and taste.

For me, the marketplace was civilized, organized, and, most of all, easy—everything the wilderness was not.

Or was it? Just as my early seasons of challenges taught me not to assume that becoming a Christian meant life would be easy, this past decade, which has been filled with uncertainty, inequality, and scarcity, has made me reconsider the ultimate safety and security of the marketplace where I spent most of my adult life.

For more than thirty years, my identity was centered on what happened in the boardroom and the corner office. And while I encountered plenty of stress and a fair amount of conflict, in general the marketplace was good to me. I found daily opportunities to bless customers and employees, and as I've shared, God blessed me in return.

However, with the benefit of distance and the harsh realities of the post-recession world, I also see that the marketplace is not regarded as a safe space for everyone. Our workplaces, economies, and systems of government are all made by humans, and as such, they reflect the imperfection and weaknesses of the human condition. Instead of honoring all of God's creation equally, human nature puts unequal values on people based on the size of their bank accounts, the color of their skin, or the name of the school they attended. Some are shut out from opportunity, while others are elevated to out-of-touch pedestals. Being on either end of the increasingly polarized spectrum has its dangers.

The ready supply of goods and capital can make those who are successful at accumulating material wealth forget that our true provision comes only from God. When things go well, the marketplace makes people believe they are sufficient on their own, and it draws attention to their own actions rather than to God's provision. Over time, many leaders of the marketplace can lose their ideals and begin to seek only their own advancement.

The Reimagine Group, the media and resource company I lead, produces short videos to help churches communicate important concepts to their congregations. Several of our video series center on a thirtysomething couple who has clearly done well in the marketplace. They have all the things money can buy—lots of savings, plenty of free time, and a mansion with a pool, a guesthouse, and a gardener. What they don't have, at least at the beginning of the series, is the understanding that everything they have is really God's and is meant to be used for his purposes, not for their own security and comfort.

I've met plenty of people like this, people who are confident in their own abilities and too busy managing their plentiful gifts to notice the needs of others. As with the rich young man who approached Jesus asking about eternal life, their possessions end up owning them instead of the other way around.

The marketplace, in this case, becomes their idol, and they spend all their time here at the expense of their personal relationships with God and his people.

On the other side of the spectrum are those who distrust the marketplace because it has somehow betrayed them or shut them out. They are judged harshly because of their gender, age, body, race, health, or where they live. The more I see how entire neighborhoods are forced to rely on payday loans and overpriced markets, or how middle-aged workers are phased out of their jobs as a cost-cutting measure, the more my perspective of the market as a "safe" place fades. This reality has shaped how I now view the marketplace versus the wilderness.

Yes, the marketplace has been my friend. It has brought countless benefits to others, not just to me. But the more I look at the wilderness—and God's place in it—the more I am challenged to consider that the marketplace has its problems. Those who find "success" often discover that it's fleeting, as a change in the market or a new innovation makes their usefulness decrease, pushing them into a new season in the wilderness.

Plenty of business leaders talk about implementing faith-based practices to address these issues of opportunity and inequality, but too often "Christian" principles of justice and mercy take back seats to the driving demands of profit and pride. Challenged by the stress of the marketplace and the demands of competition, they lose sight of the balance between justice and mercy and use any excuse to justify poor treatment of employees and predatory behavior toward customers as "just business." I, myself, struggled at times with the constant pressures from customers, employees, and shareholders. Finding a just and compassionate way to serve all of them was never easy.

God is present in the marketplace, but the truth is that the scarcity mind-set is also rooted there. It too is a difficult place to live; it is full of struggle and temptation. Every day is a chance to overcome temptation or give in to it. The danger of living in the wilderness is more obvious, and its painful effects are more immediately felt. Yet it is also where God and his abundance reside. He waits for us in the places that demand our attention, energy, and emotion. In the wilderness, it is immediately obvious how little we have and how dependent we are on God. There is no question of self-sufficiency. God gives us the wilderness because that is where our lives change and where we often find the most genuine and authentic relationships.

Again, from Bill Lawrence's book *Wilderness Wanderings*:

The wilderness is God's original temple, His personal dwelling place where He called His followers out to meet

Him and be in His presence. It was in the wilderness that God called and commissioned Moses, and gave him the Ten Commandments. Here, God formed Israel and guided Moses to create the tabernacle. The wilderness also was where God prepared David to be king of His nation and the prototype of His Son. God met with His prophet Elijah and prepared His prophet John the Baptist in the wilderness. The Holy Spirit drove Jesus into the wilderness to be tested, tempted, and proven as Messiah. Scripture also tells that Paul's theological thinking was fashioned and finalized in the wilderness.[2]

God's provision is inextricably linked to our faith and active dependence on living in his will, which builds relationship. And our dependence on him develops and grows in times of need.

God never promised the Israelites that things would be easy after they left Egypt. And he never said he would protect us from our own wildernesses. According to Deuteronomy 8:2, Moses took his people to the wilderness to humble and test them to discover what was in their hearts and whether they would keep God's commands. Too often, I have failed that test. I have been selfish and willful, and many of my prayers during those early years in the wilderness were requests for God to make things better, to incrementally change them. I wanted God to give me grace and power by *delivering* me from the wilderness.

But looking back, I don't think that's what God wanted me to see in those trials. Instead, God promised me a place to meet him even in the barren, directionless, life-altering wilderness of my major life changes and loss. God's grace and power come *in the midst of weakness.* That is abundance, but not of the sort we normally desire.

Plenty of resources today show people of faith how to impact the marketplace. But if we are truly going to reap the reward of God's abundance and live in the ways he describes in Scripture, then we need to also think about the opposite. It's more important to show people in the marketplace how to experience God in the wilderness.

Shut Down and Shut Out

For many Americans, there have been no challenges greater than the ones we faced as a nation in the aftermath of the September 11 attacks. In September 2001, I was the CEO and cofounder of a large corporate travel company. We had grown rapidly, and on the morning of 9/11, we had five thousand employees and a payroll of more than $600,000 per day. Our primary business came from booking airline tickets. When the Twin Towers fell, planes stopped flying and our revenue was cut off.

Our competitors reacted swiftly, cutting staffing by about 25 percent overnight. One well-known parking company furloughed all its drivers without pay.

My chairman called from Europe to ask what I was going to do. I thought about all the families who depended on the paychecks we provided and said, "Nothing, until we come up with a plan." I let the employees, who were understandably nervous, know we would not cut any jobs or implement any pay cuts until we had a better take on how best to move forward. It took three weeks, and during this period, I did something I had never done before. I invited all our employees to join a conference call, which I opened with a short prayer. I invoked God to give us his wisdom and favor, and then I prayed for his protection for our staff as well as for our country, our leadership, the victims, and their families.

Our company had a diverse workforce, and I'd never used "God talk" unless I felt the Holy Spirit opening an individual's heart. I'd certainly never prayed in front of the entire staff. Yet during this time of national mourning and uncertainty, I wanted to be honest and let them know I did not have any answers. I didn't know what to do other than rely on God during such a time.

Piece by piece, a plan came together. With the approval and support of our bank and our board, we bought a large competitor in order to "right-size" revenue. While our profits were wiped out for a year, we were poised for future growth and were able to keep all but 7 percent of our staff while our average competitor cut over 20 percent of staff. And we added many new clients who cited the way we treated our workforce as a reason they wanted to work with us.

When we do not have enough, whether it's in our personal lives or in our workplaces, it's natural to shut down and shut people out, the way so many businesses did in the frightening aftermath of 9/11. The marketplace offered no answers, but by staying in the wilderness and seeking God there, we were able to navigate a solution that honored our faithful staff and acknowledged God's sovereignty.

I may not like it when I'm going through it, but the wilderness is where I am changed. It is where I learn to let go of my fear. It is where God steps in to reveal a new way of living that pushes me past the scarcity mentality of the marketplace.

Living in the Wilderness

When I was a young man, not yet a Christian, I played a lot of poker. Some of the lessons I learned from those hands of cards still apply. For instance, one of the keys to a successful game of poker is perspective. You can't control what hand you're dealt. You may get great cards that make you feel unbeatable. You may get a terrible hand that doesn't add up to anything. In an average game, both of those things will happen more than once. But the reality is that sometimes the "unbeatable" hands still lose, and if you bluff just right, a bad hand can still win. A smart poker player knows how to look at each hand as an opportunity, no matter what it looks like on the surface.

In the thirty-eight years since my sister-in-law Lauri contracted polio, she has had a remarkable journey. She became a Christian and now thanks God for drawing her to him through the hardship of her situation. Her condition requires around-the-clock care, plus wheelchairs, specially modified vans, and assistance with every chore and part of life. To put it mildly, Lauri's life can be expensive. She received only $200,000 in a settlement related to her polio, which is not very much money when it comes to caring for a quadriplegic. Yet after all this time, her account still has sufficient funds to meet her needs. Her situation reminds me of the biblical story of the Israelites, whose shoes miraculously never wore out during forty years of wandering in the wilderness.

While the hand Lauri was dealt may not look like much at first glance, she says being in a wheelchair has taught her to "look up" to God. She has an ongoing ministry to the caregivers who work with her.

Like Lauri, Lisa and I both have a more dependent relationship with God because of what we've been through, which is what I asked God for in Australia. Out of death and loss comes amazing power. Every pain, disappointment, and failure in our lives has the potential to create a new raw material that, with enough time and pressure, can be used by God to make something wholly new and miraculous.

The Place Where God Provides

Is this just a big rationalization? Will God really provide something redeemable through the tragedy or gut-wrenching uncertainty that drove you to this book? I would say yes and no.

Yes, he will provide. No, it may not be what you expect.

What are the losses you face right now? The loss of a loved one? A financial loss? The loss of your home? The loss of your reputation? The loss of your health? The death of a dream? God can, over time, make those into assets for his kingdom and your provision.

That doesn't mean he's going to magically make things "better" if we pray the right prayer or do the right deed. Our interpretation of what is "right" often isn't the same as what God sees, and most of us who have been to the wilderness have shaken our fists at God and accused him of not keeping up his side of the bargain to be loving and faithful. I certainly have.

People prayed for Lauri to be healed of her polio or to regain her mobility. But God's provision for Lauri came *through* her worst circumstance, not in its absence.

When God seems to "go over the line," the situation can trigger even more brokenness, hard-heartedness, or both.

People grow bitter at their circumstances, which paralyzes their ability to look for a different perspective or a better way to play the hand they've been dealt.

Jesus never promised us an easy life. In fact, he specifically warned we would face persecution and pain if we followed him. But the Bible also assures us that God is all-wise and all-loving. We can trust his heart, even during times of pain and adversity. That's an easy thing to say but a difficult thing to live out and believe day to day. Yet in exchange for short-term discomfort, God gives us the promise of an eternity of abundance.

After we invoke God and invite him into the details of our lives, he reorders and repurposes us. From this reordering our future provision comes. But our faith is often tested. This is the type of testing that is summed up by Job: "The LORD gave and the LORD has taken away; may the name of the LORD be praised" (Job 1:21).

This testing is more complicated than making a choice between the marketplace and the wilderness. God extends his grace and provision in both. But the wilderness is where he calls us to voluntarily visit to find those who most need our love. This is an idea we will explore more in the next chapter.

Before we can consider the opportunity of reaching others, we first need to make friends with the wilderness, since it is one of the places where we can access God and his provision. Often, the wilderness provides more of a one-on-one experience with God where we deal with him directly. The marketplace, in contrast, is far more nuanced. It is easy to see growth as God's favor and failure as his lack of blessing. I have been deceived, as have others, to equate success and notoriety with favor from God.

Making Friends with the Wilderness

Being open to the wilderness means accepting the death of what's familiar. Spiritually, Jesus cited the same truth when he said, "Unless a kernel of wheat falls to the ground and dies, it remains only a single seed. But if it dies, it produces many seeds" (John 12:24). Every seed has a hard shell that needs to break. I believe people do as well. When we're willing to open ourselves to God's direction, even when it leads to uncomfortable places, we are left with his great promises: that he will never leave us nor forsake us, that nothing can separate us from his love, and that, as Paul writes in Romans 8:18, "our present sufferings are not worth comparing with the glory that will be revealed in us."

We've talked about imagining ourselves as raw materials, mere silica in the sand of God's kingdom, and about being willing to lay everything we have on the table for his use. But silica doesn't reach its full capacity as the centerpiece of our electronic devices until it has been burned in a fire as hot as the lava that shoots from a volcano. Without heat, silica is simply beach sand, and without the challenges of the wilderness, we are not refined and tested, ready to give up everything for God's sake. When we live for only ourselves and our own pleasure, we are not ready for his service.

Perhaps this is why Jesus regularly took the disciples to the wilderness. They stopped on hillsides full of hungry people and bordered by angry seas; they talked to the sick and the outcasts and to self-righteous religious zealots. Every time, the disciples wavered in their faith. They could not see how God would provide.

The disciples are not alone. The Israelites often lost faith in God, even while in their Promised Land. They wanted to go back to the easy irrigation of Egypt. Yet it was in the Promised Land, the place of full reliance on God, that they could throw off the shackles of scarcity and embrace the abundance of their God.

As Christians, we have the opportunity to learn from the disciples and the Israelites. We have the chance to look differently at the hand God has dealt us.

So we must ask ourselves, Do we believe God is for us? Do we believe he will allow painful things to happen during our lives—which are just fragments of his eternity—to accomplish the greater good for his kingdom and those he loves?

If we are unwilling to accept that our time in the wilderness is part of God's plan, and to look for his presence even there, then we will always have a limited experience of God's provision. But if we are willing to follow God wherever he leads, then we set the stage for new growth and provision.

God's Rhythm of Provision for You: Challenges

The wilderness, while a difficult and scary place at times, serves an important purpose in God's plan of provision. In challenges, God turns on the furnace to convert the silica of our lives and character into something else—silicon. This is where the miracle of transformation takes place. Remember that without the challenges of the wilderness, we are not properly tested or transformed.

In Daniel 3, we see God join Shadrach, Meshach, and Abednego in the fiery furnace. As you think about the challenges you face, ask God to make his presence known to you in the furnace, especially when you don't feel his presence. Think of his promise in Matthew 28:20, "Surely I am with you always, to the very end of the age," and pray that God will reveal himself to you in a special way in your trial.

In the area of challenges, evaluate yourself on a scale of 1 to 10:

① When I have trials, I think God, if he exists, does not love me. I cannot get over my anger and discouragement.

⑤ I try to persevere in my trials, but I still struggle with seeing good or purpose coming out of these challenges.

⑩ I believe I need to make friends with the wilderness and to see that this reordering of my life is part of God's plan.

Your score: _____

Enter your score on page 211.

6

Choosing the Wilderness

Growing in the Challenges

As a businessman, I am fascinated by numbers—especially what the finance community calls "returns and rewards." What happens after we make an investment? What do we receive for taking a risk?

These aren't just questions for the marketplace. Four times in Scripture Jesus is recorded as actually giving a numerical return for certain activities.

For the first instance, we look again at the parable of the bags of gold. Matthew 25 recounts Jesus telling a story about three servants who each receive bags of gold from their master to steward while he is away. Two of the three servants—those who are given five bags and two bags of gold—risk everything they are given and end up doubling their initial stake. This was no small investment. Scholars estimate the value of each bag of gold, or what the King

James Version calls a "talent," at as much as twenty years' worth of wages for a common worker. These servants made investments that brought back more than they could reasonably expect to make in their lifetimes. (And the servant who made the most was also given the gold of the third servant, who had hidden the one bag of gold the master had given him rather than using it. That's another twenty years of income!)

"Well done, good and faithful servant," the master says. "You have been faithful with a few things; I will put you in charge of many things. Come and share your master's happiness!" (Matthew 25:21). For the servants who understood the heart of their master and risked everything for him, the return was eternal life.

We find a second, somewhat parallel parable in Luke 19:11–27. The master in this case gives each servant one mina, the equivalent of three months' wages. When the master returns, the first servant reports he has turned one mina into ten. He is rewarded with ten cities, which we can interpret to mean additional authority and responsibility in heaven. The second servant has turned one mina into five and is given five cities. And again, one servant has acted in fear. Misunderstanding the heart and desire of his master, he hid away what he was given. His mina is taken away and given to the man with ten cities.

We find a third set of numbers in Matthew 13:1–23 in the parable of the sower. Jesus describes the Word of God as a seed that is sown in four kinds of soil, representing human hearts. How open are our hearts to truth? When the Word is spread where there is no soil or on rocky soil or among thorns, there is little or no return. But when the seed falls on good soil, there is a crop "a hundred, sixty or thirty times what was sown" (v. 8).

Over and over, we see God rewarding those who take risks, who know the heart of the master, and who have hearts that are open to truth. He punishes those who allow the cares of this world and the deceitfulness of riches to choke out fruitfulness in God's kingdom.

This all leads us to the remarkable nature of one final passage of Scripture concerning returns. In Matthew 19:27, Peter says to Jesus, "We have left everything to follow you! What then will there be for us?" Peter and the other disciples had given up everything they had—families, careers, homes, and, increasingly, their safety—for Jesus. Now Peter wants to know what they will get for it. Jesus answers him, "At the renewal of all things, when the Son of Man sits on his glorious throne, you who have followed me will also sit on twelve thrones, judging the twelve tribes of Israel" (Matthew 19:28). For their sacrifice, he says, the people who have followed him "will receive a hundred times as much and will inherit eternal life" (Matthew 19:29). Isn't it interesting that the highest return cited by Jesus (100 times) went to those who left or lost the dearest people or things in their lives?

We know God calls us to go willingly into hard places. Jesus said as much when he stated that every seed must die before it bears fruit. The bread and fish had to be broken before they became practical provision for a hungry crowd. And we must be willing to put ourselves on the line and take God-directed risks to expand his kingdom.

But it's important to remember that these experiences must be measured in light of eternity. Scripture shows us four times that in Jesus's calculation of returns and rewards, "the books" are not closed in a single human lifetime. They last for eternity, where his everlasting love is the highest return we could possibly receive. He will wipe away every tear, love us with his everlasting love, and give the highest return on our lives.

How we live through the wilderness experiences of this life demonstrates the highest call of the kingdom—what I call our "stewardship of loss." God calls us to manage and care for not only our finances, time, and talents but also our pain, losses, and weaknesses. We don't talk about this call nearly enough, but this is where the wilderness changes us.

Everyday Disruption

Let's look again at the marketplace. In business, growth and innovation require disruption and change. Most break-throughs start with what I call a "discontinuous vision or idea." Your company can't keep doing things the same way, year after year, if the world is changing around it.

When I was a teenager, I used to go door-to-door selling copies of the Encyclopedia Britannica. At the time, this was the most authoritative source of information available to the general public, and displaying a full set of leather-bound volumes on your bookshelf was a status symbol—and an expensive one. Thirty years ago, a full set of encyclopedias cost more than $1,000. But time passed, and when the digital age came, information became much easier to access. Micro-soft released a digital encyclopedia for less than $100. Today most people turn to free sources such as Wikipedia or Google. Unable to compete with these digital sources, Encyclopedia Britannica stopped printing books in 2010.

Over at the Eastman Kodak Company, known as Kodak, a similar story was unfolding. Through most of the twentieth century, Kodak was the runaway leader and patent holder for amateur photography and film. In 1975, Steve Sasson, a Kodak engineer, invented the first electronic camera. His bosses were unimpressed. Why would they want to change the way people processed photos? Film was a cash cow for them; just like every razor needs blades, every camera needed film. And every camera owner was a captive customer needing to develop that film. Their product wouldn't work without Kodak's development services.

Kodak shelved Sasson's invention, but others were working on similar projects. By the early twenty-first century, consumers had shifted almost entirely to digital cameras made by other companies. By the time Kodak began producing digital camera equipment, it was too late. The company filed for bankruptcy in 2012.[1]

But embracing discontinuity requires courage. Sometimes taking risks doesn't work out the way we expect. When I first got into the travel business, I had an idea to start a travel club and sell memberships through TV. I hired a nationally famous spokesperson and called the venture Grand Style Vacations. Our core business was corporate travel, and I thought this was a sure way to innovate and expand our company. The idea, however, never took off. The travel club went bust, and I ended up with a very expensive handful of Grand Style Vacations T-shirts.

What does this have to do with you? Chances are you're not a business owner facing possible extinction. But you are a person who has a choice, every day, to follow the tried-and-true path of safety, which can lead to stagnation and scarcity, or to take a risk and walk into the wilderness God is showing you.

The wilderness is the lab where God sends us to grow and innovate, where we meet new people and become new people. As Deuteronomy 8:2 says, this is the land that tests us to show us what is in our hearts.

To continue to reap returns—or, in terms of a personal context, to receive God's full provision—we must be willing not only to accept our personal wilderness when he leads us there but also to *seek out* the uncomfortable places where we can serve others. In business language, we must be willing to innovate and risk our capital—our time, experiences, and resources.

And that means being open to and aware of our own challenges as well as the challenges of others. God will provide as we lean in to our most difficult areas and love and serve others.

Fatherless Boys

In 2001, I was part of a small group of men who met weekly to talk about our lives, the Bible, and the places where those overlapped.

Just a few months after we began meeting, one of the men, George, announced to the group that he had taken a major step of faith. "This week," George said, "I prayed, and I asked Jesus to take over and to be the Lord of my life. For the first time, I feel a real assurance that I belong to him."

I was amazed and thrilled that God had brought something so meaningful out of our group. But then, just a few months later, I received a devastating phone call. George, who had suffered with depression for years, had committed suicide.

I couldn't believe it. Not George. He had asked Jesus to be the Lord of his life! How could this happen? Was there a clue I had missed? Had I failed him? Had I failed God?

When I went to the funeral home to offer my condolences, George's widow and two sons were in a room with a number of mourners and supporters. George's older son, Rob, went to school and played on the golf team with one of my sons, so I had met the family before. But that day it was the sight of George's younger son, Kevin, just twelve years old, that shook me deeply.

He was almost the same age I had been when my father had died.

I stayed in touch with the family, especially the boys. And then one day Rob invited me to attend the father-son weekend at his college. I accepted, humbled and honored that he had invited me into his wilderness.

That weekend retreat was the beginning of what became a rich mentoring relationship between me and George's sons— a relationship that has taught and benefited me as much as it has them. I played golf with them, we opened our home to them on school holidays, and over the years they have often come to me for life advice, career guidance, and spiritual counsel. Today they're both strong young men who love Jesus. When Rob got married, he invited my wife and me to sit at the family table.

This was the beginning of a new and unexpected ministry for me. My own sons were grown, but I became aware that there were many fatherless boys who needed a man to join them in their wildernesses. In time, the Lord brought two other boys into my life—Antonio, who had been abandoned by his father, and Pierce, who had watched his father die a painful death from a rare wasting disease.

Over the course of two weeks, Pierce's father, Scott, lost his ability to walk, became blind, and then died. Pierce was only eight years old. Scott's wife, Pam, called me shortly after he died and asked if I would mentor Pierce, the second child in their family of four boys.

Once again, I entered the world of mentoring the fatherless. I attended after-school track meets, took him out to breakfast, and offered advice when he needed it. The most meaningful experience for me came when Pierce was fourteen, and we stood sixty feet above the ground at a Northern California father-son camp. The counselors called it a "ropes" course, but to me it looked more like a "very thin wire" course. Pierce and I needed to traverse two parallel cables, set three feet apart, keeping our balance by holding each other's hands and leaning on each other. To make things worse, there were obstacles between us.

I assessed the risk and thought there was only a small chance we would make it. Physics was not on our side. I outweighed Pierce by more than a hundred pounds, not to mention the fifty-year age difference.

"We can do it, Jack!" Pierce's youthful enthusiasm broke through my doubt. I took his hands and stepped out onto the wire.

One step at a time, we made our way through the challenge.

I cannot begin to list all the gifts God has given me as I have walked through life with these four boys as well as with my own three sons. Each time I entered one of their wildernesses, I reentered one of my own. And with each experience,

I found incredible healing in a place that had felt like a bleak wasteland for many years.

It is difficult to embrace loss and failure. But when we do, God can use the experience for our good.

Everyone who has lived for a few decades in a broken world has areas of their lives that they feel should be off-limits to everyone, even to God. These are the tender areas of our hearts, the places we fear may break if we touch them. But often, these are the very wilderness places God calls us to use to serve others.

Part of our own healing and provision comes as we take risks and open ourselves to change, voluntarily entering the wildernesses of other people's lives.

A Matter of Perspective

Jordan Spieth is a professional golfer on the PGA Tour who has been ranked as the number one player in the Official World Golf Ranking. He has also made *Time*'s "100 Most Influential People" list, in which he was described as someone who "exemplifies everything that's good about sports."[2]

As I've watched Spieth play, one thing that has stood out to me is that in every interview, he refers to his success using terms such as "we" and "our team." That's unusual in an individual sport like golf. But Spieth is quick to point out that his parents, his caddy, his coaches, and his advisers all bring something to his game. And more than any of them, Spieth credits as his "key inspiration" his sister Ellie, who is autistic. He goes to hug her first after every win. In an interview, he said, "I try to get back home all the time to be with her and regroup. . . . She sets everything in perspective for me. She is so happy for the littlest of things."[3]

The "wilderness" of Ellie's situation grounds Spieth, a talented young man who could easily lose himself in the spotlight. But he knows life is about more than winning a game.

In my current filmmaking ventures, I've learned a lot from the talented team that writes, directs, acts in, and edits our work. One of the key things I've discovered is this: a film is more than a single frame. Our initial idea may involve a single dramatic image, or there might be one great line of dialogue, but what really matters is how it all works *together*.

Our lives are like movies. A single frame of our lives may seem blindingly bright, like a PGA Tour win. Or it may be bleak, bordering on hopeless. Ominous shadows may lurk all around the image—the threat of a devastating storm. But we must remember these are only single frames of a much larger work of art. God can already see the entire movie, and he alone knows how those shadows of disappointment and loss will affect the future.

When life slaps us with wilderness experiences, they are almost always untimely and unwanted. The stress of a loved one's death or a job loss can keep us awake at night. Particular events can seem to dominate our entire world. But if we remember these are single frames in a greater story, they can also reorient us toward the eternal things that really matter. In the end, our homes, our careers, and even our families are temporary. Only God is eternal. Only he knows how a particular season will change our lives—and the lives of others—for eternity.

Losing my father when I was a child was devastating. But when I look back with perspective and see how it prepared me to make a difference in the lives of seven young men, I consider that loss in a new way. My wilderness was used for God's purposes.

What Happens When We Show Up

Many years ago, I was a manager in a company in which certain people had built up power bases for themselves by forming alliances with one another. It was a toxic environment full of gossip and relationships that were made to damage others and destroy careers. One woman in particular took advantage of her position to access the business and personal files of the leadership team, including me. She began gossiping about me, spreading lies and innuendos. Others got involved, and the office became a miserable, dangerous place to be every day.

At first, I got angry. I was determined to defend myself and set the record straight, but those defensive plans got tangled in my feelings of hatred. As an officer of the company, I kept thinking, *I have the right to fire these people.*

But drowning out those thoughts were the words of Christ: "Love your enemies and pray for those who persecute you" (Matthew 5:44).

I'm glad I heard those words, but frankly, I preferred hearing them in my devotions rather than in the heat of battle, especially when the goal of that battle was personal. I wanted justice. I wanted revenge.

But God didn't give up. He kept knocking on the door of my heart, pleading for me to forgive instead of fight back. Against my will, I began to pray for the situation and the people involved. I started to reach out to the woman who had entrenched herself against me. I began including her in planning meetings, asking her advice on various matters, and trying to be positive and proactive.

For a while, nothing changed. But then one day something amazing happened. The woman came to me with a picture of herself taken years earlier. "This is me," she said, showing me a woman who was considerably heavier. Suddenly, the barriers of mistrust came down. And with the barriers, the hatred collapsed as well. I realized she was reaching out to me for understanding, compassion, and, perhaps, forgiveness.

The entire experience remains a painful chapter in my life, but it is also a joyful memory, because it reminds me of God's power to turn our selfish hearts into generous ones as we meditate on his merciful love for us.

These kinds of opportunities to offer kindness and hope come up more often than we might think. While I was working on this chapter, my wife, Lisa, mentioned she was going over to a friend's house. Her friend is a hoarder and had recently told Lisa her daughter did not have a clear space anymore to do her homework. Lisa stepped into that immediate wilderness and spent a whole day clearing out just one room, the dining room, so this family would have a place to eat and work. The friend cried tears of joy when the project was finished.

Or consider this. A friend and business acquaintance recently lost his wife. Instead of picking up the phone or sending him an email to talk about some projects we're working on, I invited him to breakfast. He lives on the other side of the city, so I spent forty minutes, each way, driving to a meeting that lasted only half an hour, just because I wanted to be present with him. I wanted to hug him, look him in the eye, and join him in his wilderness.

There was a time when I never would have done that. When my identity was wrapped up in the marketplace, I used to put dollar values on every minute of my time. I talked about prioritizing, outsourcing, and multitasking. I factored the expense of stopping to pick up my own dry cleaning, thinking I could be doing something more valuable. But what God has shown me time after time is that nothing is more valuable than what he calls me to do—and whom he calls me to serve. If we approach the wilderness with mindful prayer, an open heart, and a servant attitude, then nothing we do in his name is too small to have value.

This idea of meeting others and joining together to accomplish God's goal is a powerful concept, one we will explore more in-depth in the next section. God has repeatedly used face-to-face encounters to bring me to deeper levels of vulnerability, to show me to trust in a new way, and to help me see him not only as my Lord but also as the innovator of my life.

What's Your Excuse?

In 1996, my hometown of Atlanta, Georgia, hosted the Olympic Games and then the subsequent Paralympic Games, in which athletes with physical disabilities compete. The advertising slogan for the Paralympics stuck with me: "What's your excuse?" The tagline was splashed across pictures of sprinters running one hundred meters with a prosthetic leg or basketball players in wheelchairs or swimmers who were missing a limb.

Around that time, I was asked to speak at the funeral of a longtime family friend whose name was Mary. I stood in front of her church and said, "Mary is in heaven right now, and she would say three words to all of us: What's your excuse?"

To my surprise, the congregation answered back, "What's our excuse?" The engagement of the congregation's call-and-response egged me on.

"Is your job your excuse?"

They answered, "Our job."

"Is your spouse your excuse?"

"Our spouse."

And so it went, for about twenty minutes.

The point is we all make excuses. We hold on to the parts of ourselves where our fears and past hurts still sting. We live in places ruled by the philosophy of scarcity, believing we don't have enough to offer to others. But those are the very places where God can use us in the deepest, most life-changing, most freedom-bringing ways. Stewarding our pain, weaknesses, losses, and failures is just as important as using our strengths and gifts—perhaps even more important.

The apostle Paul said that God's power is made perfect in weakness (2 Corinthians 12:9). What if, like the Paralympic heroes, we could each harness the power behind our weakness?

The wilderness for most of my life represented the places where I felt alone and afraid. It represented death, disability, loss, and the total lack of control. Only when I started to make friends with the idea of a wilderness where God can give to me rather than take from me did I find the abundance he offers to all who come to him.

To fully understand God's provision, we must handle our challenges and enter other people's wildernesses. Only when we are willing to see the capacity of the loneliest places and consecrate to him the things that seem most hopeless on the surface can he truly and completely use us. Is all this easy? No. It's possible only when we rely on God's strength, depend on his grace, and engage a community to support us.

When God breaks things, he does so with a purpose. You may not be able to recognize that purpose right now, but God wants to turn your loss into an asset that will bless others. Understanding this concept is probably one of the hardest things you will do in your life. But it's also the most meaningful. Your pain holds untapped power—power that can change far more lives than just your own.

God's Rhythm of Provision for You: Growing in Challenges

Pain and passion are often "first cousins." The trite phrase is that we each have a chance to "be bitter or better," but we can't really be better without understanding God's love or plan.

Earlier in this book, we talked about finished products and raw materials. We can intellectually acknowledge that most products we buy must go through the manufacturing process of separation (consecration) and purification (challenges). Parts 2 and 3 of this book showed that the physical processes actually mirror the spiritual growth that God wants to take us through.

Pray and ask God to give you a new perspective on your pain and challenges. Ask him to turn your pain into passion to serve someone else.

In the area of growing in challenges, evaluate yourself on a scale of 1 to 10:

1 My pain has been too great. I have a hard time getting past it.

5 I am still struggling but have seen too many instances of things turning around for people who have failed or suffered great loss.

10 I see myself as a raw material and that God has a plan to refine me for his glory. I do not always understand his plan, and I do not like the refining process, but I trust him.

1	2	3	4	5	6	7	8	9	10

Your score: _____

Enter your score on page 211.

Part 4

COMMUNITY

Jesus then took the loaves, gave thanks, and *distributed to those who were seated* as much as they wanted. He did the same with the fish.

John 6:11, emphasis added

7

Check Your Orbit

The Role of Community

One of the most memorable rounds of golf I ever played was in Castle Pines, Colorado. A client invited me to play in a prestigious Pro-Am golf tournament in which four amateurs play eighteen holes with a professional golfer. At the "draw party" the night before, I found out I would play with Jack Nicklaus, arguably the greatest golfer of all time.

I didn't sleep very well that night, but the next morning I played a delightful eighteen holes with one of my heroes. Fans lined each fairway and crowded around every green. As we got to the eighteenth hole, there was quite a gallery. The crowd started chanting, "Jack! Jack! Jack!"

I stood a bit taller as I surveyed the crowd and took it all in.

Of course, about half a second later, I realized the crowd's adoration was not directed at me. Those people cared about a different Jack.

For as long as humans have lived outside the Garden of Eden, we've struggled with the temptation to see ourselves as the center of the universe and the star of the play. That sense of self-importance can sneak up on us when we least expect it, even when we're trying to act with the best intentions.

In my years as a corporate executive, I had the responsibility to hire, fire, and pay people, so it's not surprising that many of them treated me with certain deference. My job title placed me in the center of their professional lives, and they treated me accordingly. I must admit that at the time the attention felt right. I saw the power of my position as part of God's blessing on me as I served him. But as I look back, I can also see how distracting, and even disorienting, all that attention was for me.

If you had asked me back then how I served God, I would have said, "I use my gifts as a businessman to build successful companies. I invest in those companies, and when I get a return on that investment, I give as much of that money away as I can to the church and worthy Christian organizations." In other words, I used *my* time, *my* talent, and *my* treasure to enlarge *my* assets, and I gave a portion of *my* assets to God to use for his kingdom.

There was a lot of *me* in that approach—and not a lot of God.

My intentions were good, but I was missing a critical piece—*the* critical piece, it turns out—of God's promise of abundance and his ultimate purpose for my life.

I didn't really understand it until God started dismantling my ideas about success and service by bringing people into my life like Pierce, the boy who needed a father figure more than he needed a check, and Natasha, who needed kindness to help heal her wounds of broken relationships as much as she needed a referral to heal her broken smile. From them, and dozens of others like them, I started to see the full picture of how God provides for his creations.

Jesus's Fourth Action

We've read about Jesus taking the bread, consecrating it, and breaking it. But the miracle was not over with those actions. Each Gospel records one more thing he did: Jesus shared his gift.

The action is so obvious that it's easy to overlook. We think, Well, of course he gave the food to the people. It wouldn't have been much of a miracle of provision if he'd held on to it for himself.

But wait. Think for a moment about how complicated it must have been to get food to fifteen thousand people. Matthew 14:19 says Jesus "gave [the loaves and fish] to the disciples, and the disciples gave them to the people."

That must have taken some time. The disciples were likely exhausted . . . and hungry. What would have happened if they, responding to the growls of their stomachs, had taken the bread from Jesus's hands and put it straight into their own mouths? What if they'd looked at what was happening as an individual miracle, a private gift for only them?

What if they had seen themselves as the center of the universe in that moment?

The full miracle would have stopped.

In other words, Jesus's abundant provision depended on the willingness of the community around him to serve and give generously to one another. And it still does.

This fourth and final aspect of God's provision draws us out of our comfort zones and into the communities around us. We are fully blessed and provided for when we bless and provide for others.

Our provision and even miracles often happen through community. Perhaps they happen through new people. New circumstances. New doors that open that we never could have imagined. We need to walk into these new relationships with faith and courage, believing that God has something new in store for us. Just as Jesus's miracle with the loaves and fish never would have occurred without the crowd, so our provision often won't happen without new people and new circumstances in our lives.

Of all the aspects of God's provision we've looked at in this book, this one is the richest because it encompasses not just our individual relationships with God the Creator but also the relationships we have with his creations.

It is also the most difficult to live out fully, especially when times are hard. Feelings of scarcity and fear encourage us to withdraw into ourselves, to limit our connections to others. But that's just the opposite of what God wants for us.

Living in Orbit

I love reading about new inventions, developments, and ways humans are exploring our capacity. One thing I've noticed is how often a human discovery is based on a principle or a design the discoverer first noticed in nature. For example, did you know the Wright brothers' airplane designs were inspired by the wings of pigeons in flight? Or that one of the inventors of the modern hypodermic needle got his idea from the sting of a bee?

The term for this imitation of natural biological designs, processes, and systems is *biomimicry*. Dozens of books and websites are dedicated to sharing stories such as how the inventor of Velcro was inspired by the way burdock burrs stuck to his dog's coat or how the incandescence of a butterfly's wing influenced color e-readers and other display technology. Polar bear fur, which is hollow to provide extra warmth and insulation in arctic winters, was the inspiration for everything from solar energy collectors to textiles for new clothing lines. The swarm behavior of bee colonies influenced multitasking internet server networks and more efficiently connected heating and cooling systems.[1]

These discoveries changed the way we live, and I suspect millions more are still waiting to be uncovered. The best human inventions mimic nature, just as we, when we are at our best, mimic the Creator who made us in his image.

That is not always an easy conclusion for people to accept. Not all inventors want to give God the credit for their ideas, just as not all humans want to acknowledge we were created as part of a divine plan and purpose. We like to think we are unique and independent creatures, at the top of earth's evolutionary chain, capable of taking care of ourselves and managing the world around us. Like toddlers who are determined to do everything themselves, we claim to be self-sufficient.

However, the key to provision is not found in our own instincts or capabilities. Provision comes only through mimicking God himself.

In his powerful book *The Reason for God*, Tim Keller unpacks the complex concept of the Trinity, the three-in-one Godhead who has confused Christians for centuries.

Keller's explanation, which has deeply influenced my thinking about the matter, is that the Trinity is primarily relational in essence, and this is where the ideal human capacity
for love and relationships comes from. The Father, the Son,
and the Holy Spirit are distinct and separate entities yet
are also dependent and interconnected—what Keller calls
"other centered." God, in his very essence and nature, is
relational.[2]

And if we live in his image, so are we.

Keller describes the mutual "love, delight, and adoration"
within the Trinity as "a dance." The early Greek church
described this interplay with the word *perichoresis*, which
became the root of our own word *choreography*, the art of
designing dance steps and movements. In this "dance," the
members of the Trinity are in a constant, interdependent
orbit. This is a picture of what we were created to do in our
relationships with God and with one another.

Back when I was in school, we learned that planets orbit
the sun and that moons orbit planets. Later, we learned that
every substance in the universe—whether solid, liquid, or
gas—is composed of atoms, and every atom has a nucleus
that is orbited by electrons. Every system, from the most
minute building blocks of life to the largest systems in the
universe, is designed to revolve around and support a central
point. If a piece of the system falls out of orbit—if a planet
stops circling a star or an electron stops circling a nucleus—
the entire nature of the system changes. We might say it no
longer has the same capacity.

Human beings too were created to orbit, only our circle
was meant to be around the Creator himself as well as the
people he created.

Before they chose sin, Adam and Eve lived solely for God. Their entire existence revolved around their time with him in the Garden of Eden and carrying out the mission he had given them. There was no pain or loss. But when they chose to disobey God—when they chose to do what they wanted rather than what he wanted—their natural orbit stopped. Sin entered the equation and brought selfishness with it.

We humans, influenced by the delusion that we are independent and separate from the Creator, started to orbit idols or, increasingly, started to expect things and people to orbit us. Narcissism grabbed ahold of us, and our sinful natures pushed us to think of only our own needs and desires.

One of the most vivid effects of that selfishness was our slow descent into secularism. After we removed the Creator from the center of our lives, it was easy to also push him out of the center of society. Christian churches used to be physically located in the center of town, right where people could see them; they were the primary channels for community development and outreach. But now it seems as if many houses of worship have become places that serve members' desire for entertainment rather than being places to connect with God and the communities around them.

Hardwired for Generosity

Because we are made in the image of God, and these ideas of relationship and community are at the core of God's being, they are hardwired into us as well.

Behavioral and neurological scientists have solid evidence that it is true: the human brain is designed for relationship

167

and generosity. God designed us to reflect the generous nature of the great Giver.

In a 2013 article in the *Wall Street Journal*, science writer Elizabeth Svoboda described new findings from the field of neuroscience. For more than a century, scientists assumed that the survival-of-the-fittest model of evolution meant that humans had been increasingly driven to compete; those who could dominate other human beings for food and mates would be most likely to pass on their genes. If this were the case, though, then how can we explain human altruism? Charles Darwin never offered a good answer. But the new research showed that generosity triggers satisfaction in the brain in the same way that our primal desires for food or even sex do. According to the article, "Where once there was only speculation about the origins of the human desire to help others, a body of data is starting to fill the gap, revealing key workings of the biological hardware that makes altruism possible."[3]

While the researchers did not draw any specific conclusions about why we humans have this unique behavior, the answer for me was clear: God designed us to give and share with others. Acts of generosity and sacrifice also appear to stimulate the production of the hormone oxytocin, which promotes bonding and closer relationships between people.

The article made me think about something that happened many years ago, when our family was part of a project to build a community center in Mexico City. It was built on a landfill, making the center a beautiful symbol of redemption as land that was once a place only for garbage was turned into a gathering place for the community.

When I went to visit the center, I met Juan, who lived across the street. He invited me to his home for dinner, and

I accepted. I could see his family was incredibly poor, yet when we sat down to eat that night, they spread a lavish meal before me. The food was wonderful, and we had an enjoyable evening of fellowship and conversation.

Later, when I mentioned the fantastic food to a friend, he said, "They are proud people, and it's important that they show you the utmost hospitality. They probably spent a third of their monthly income on that one meal."

I was shocked and humbled. At great personal sacrifice, these people had shared with me out of their essence, not merely their excess. Truly, they had no excess to spare, yet the act of giving filled them with joy.

We were made to be generous orbiters of one another.

An Orbiting Adventure

In 2002, God started a new work in my life. And he started, as he often does, by dismantling the idols, such as relationships and work, in which I found security and that were keeping me from fully engaging with him.

The new work began with a meeting with my boss, the chairman of our company. In fifteen years, we had grown the company from the two of us to more than six thousand employees. Now he said he wanted to double the size of the organization again and take it global. The opportunity was there, and I agreed the company was in a good position to grow, but my heart was not in it.

I left that meeting knowing I could not do what my boss wanted. After the suicide of my friend George, I had struggled with depression and exhaustion. I didn't have the emotional resources at the time to run two companies and oversee this kind of intense expansion while also investing in the growing number of people God was bringing into my life. I got down on my knees and prayed, "Lord, I want more of you and more of your kingdom."

Following God's prompting, I resigned from my job without a sure plan of what to do next. The only thing I knew was that I had been creating strategies to help the businesses I ran become successful. Now I heard God saying, "Jack, I want you to use your skills to help other people become successful."

I tried a few things, but nothing worked out well. Then I heard a message from Kevin Myers, the senior pastor at 12Stone Church in Georgia, that changed my life and redirected my own orbit. Myers's message was called "Cup, Sleeve, and Napkin." Here's a quick summary.

If you go to Starbucks and order a latte, the barista will serve it to you in a sturdy paper cup. Around that cup will be a sleeve to protect your hand from the heat of the coffee. And paper napkins are always available to mop up any spills.

Using Myers's metaphor, I saw how most of us, when we think about how God will use us, imagine ourselves as a coffee cup, ready to be filled with opportunity and influence. We pray for chances to lead, for platforms, and for wealth, all so we can use them to help others and advance the kingdom. We may start to see ourselves as invaluable. After all, everyone who wants coffee needs a cup. Where would God's "coffee" be without us?

But God doesn't always want us to be a coffee cup. Some of us are sleeves—those recycled paper wraps that make the cup easier to hold. That sleeve has only one job—to support the cup. It's not critical to the coffee-drinking experience, although it does make things smoother and better. Sometimes God doesn't want us to be the person with the platform and the attention; sometimes our purpose is to support someone else as they step up.

It can be humbling to be a sleeve, but there's a third type of service that gets even less recognition. Some servants in God's kingdom may never touch the coffee at all. They're the ones in the background who always seem to be cleaning up other people's messes. They're invisible to most of us—serving God and their communities quietly and out of sight day after day. They never get any credit for the work they do, yet they are invaluable to God. These, of course, are the napkins. Jesus said the greatest among the disciples were the servants, but the first in his kingdom were the slaves (Matthew 20:26–27).

Many of us are anxious to be a cup. Some of us are humble enough to be a sleeve, supporting the cup and taking the heat. But very few people are so committed to becoming like Jesus that they volunteer to be a napkin—willing to be disposed of and thrown away in the service of others.

This idea of supporting others and cleaning up their messes rattled my very being. I realized the napkin's role is really the most important of all.

My days as a cup (leader) seemed to be over, and my days as a napkin and a sleeve (servant) were just beginning.

For most of my life, I'd considered myself an opportunist. I knew how to evaluate circumstances and networks and spot opportunities for myself. But now I was being called to look at life in the opposite way: to seek awareness of opportunities for others and to be just as creative on their behalf, regardless of the personal outcome. I called it "disadvantaging" myself. God had given me the seeds of other gifts and skills that would germinate, but only if I was willing to trust him and plant them.

Lisa experienced four years of illness at about this time with a disorder that caused her to cycle between anxiety and depression. She needed me to care for and serve her, and I made this my first priority. A highlight of our marriage is the day when she hugged me and said, "You have been such a great napkin."

Instead of investing in companies and looking for financial gain, I started to serve organizations I believed in, asking for nothing in return unless they were pleased with the results. I partnered with ministries that were suffering from crippling debt and with friends who had good ideas but no management experience, using the business skills God had given me to now serve others.

Year after year, I built new relationships. I earned some bonuses, which paid my family's living costs. And I learned something every day about orbiting in community.

Reflecting God's Light

As I walked down that fairway in Colorado, I saw an example of what happens when a small figure—me, in this case—happens to orbit a much brighter figure, a central object. On that golf course, I was not the center. Yet when the crowd saw me, I reflected some of the brilliance of the much more famous Jack, much like the moon reflects the light of the sun.

In our best moments, humans are merely reflections of a brighter center. And my real role was never to be at the center of anyone's universe. Instead, I was to be a humble orbiter of a center brighter than I could ever imagine.

These days, when I meet someone with plenty of money or influence, especially if they are a Christian, I often ask how they view the gifts they have been given. Are they concerned their position will tempt them to become self-reliant or to start thinking of themselves as their own "sun"? Most people, to be honest, respond without much obvious concern. As I did, back when I felt self-important, they see their money and power as gifts, not hindrances. Those who are well versed in the lingo of the church talk about their blessings and how God has used their positions to give them "platforms" for the kingdom.

This idea of a platform as a way to describe a person's influence or reach has been popular for many years. A person with a large platform is familiar to and generally trusted by many people and has the opportunity to use that reputation to promote whatever is important to them.

Not long after I became a Christian in Australia, I met a drummer in a rock band. He too was a new believer, and his band had released a song that became a worldwide hit. Overnight, this young man went from an obscure artist to a globally known and in-demand musician.

The drummer had a desire to go to Bible school to deepen his faith, but other, more experienced Christians were trying to convince him that staying in the band would give him an incredible platform to share his faith in Christ. They told him this was a once-in-a-lifetime opportunity for the king-dom. They perhaps even implied it was selfish not to step into the spotlight.

Ultimately, though, the drummer realized that seeking God's will, not the opinions of the people around him, was the correct answer. He prayed, and God showed him that trying to leverage his platform of music when he was still such a young Christian would threaten his sense of significance and identity.

Certainly, platforms can be used for good. Not every musician will receive the same call my friend did. Actors turn their movie careers into opportunities to raise awareness about serious global crises or social issues. Business leaders use their influence to set policies based on their values, influencing employees, shareholders, customers, and the public.

The troublesome thing is that most platforms, when we think about the word literally, are bolted to the stage. They *do not move*. I find that detail to be telling. If we spend too much time thinking about the thing that keeps us bolted to one place, it's hard to orbit the One who is really at the center of all things.

Think about the word *community*. It is derived from the Latin word *communis*, which means "things held in common." The equality and the respect in that word push aside all the self-important distractions of platforms, wealth, or "deserved" influence. You cannot be the center of your own universe and still share a heart of love and service.

An Others-Focused Perspective

When I was growing up, if my mother and I were in town and we'd see someone in need, she'd pass by and pretend not to notice them. She would justify doing so by quoting Genesis 4:9: "Am I my brother's keeper?" She used this verse to limit her obligations to people around her. I didn't realize at the time—and maybe she didn't either—that these words were first said by Adam and Eve's oldest son, Cain, when he was trying to cover up that he'd just killed his brother, Abel. His insincerity was punished.

God does, in fact, call us to be our brothers' keepers: "Carry each other's burdens," writes Paul in Galatians 6:2, "and in this way you will fulfill the law of Christ."

This deep and rich commandment is at the heart of God's plan for our provision. His counterintuitive key to living a life of abundance is not about knowing the right prayers so we can receive more material goods. It's about discovering the truth that we were created to orbit the Creator.

This was a powerful lesson for me to learn. The lesson began one night in 2005 when I saw a special TV report about the effects of a devastating drought plaguing Southeast Asia. I heard for the first time that every thirty minutes, somewhere in India, another farmer reached a point of despair—usually due to deep debt and failing crops—and took his own life, sometimes by drinking the pesticides that had failed to save his harvest.

For a brief time, the world took notice of this tragedy. PBS broadcast a *Frontline* documentary called "Seeds of Suicide: India's Desperate Farmers." Other networks reported on the epidemic. But within weeks, the networks were chasing other stories, and the Indian farmers were largely forgotten.

Only, I couldn't forget them. When I saw the initial report, my heart went out to the farmers' families. No one helped them after the death of their loved ones. The widows, usually members of the "untouchable" caste and therefore already outcasts, suffered deep financial hardship as well as grief. It was not unusual to see such desperate women trafficked for sex or enslaved in some way, often by those in their own communities.

My heart was drawn, seemingly inexplicably, to these Indian widows and their children. I found a Christian organization that provided food, medical aid, shelter, and school supplies for thousands of Indian women and their children and joined the team that financially supported their work. I received regular, encouraging stories from local pastors who created job training and support programs and visited the women frequently, offering unconditional support and love.

Several times over the following ten years, the ministry invited me to go to India to see the work and personally meet the families. While my compassion was genuine, I didn't feel called to go. I made excuses about not having time, the cost, and not wanting to draw attention to myself.

Then one day I heard a sermon on Genesis 12, where God says to Abraham, "I will make you into a great nation, and I will bless you; I will make your name great, and you will be a blessing. I will bless those who bless you, and whoever curses you I will curse; and all peoples on earth will be blessed through you" (vv. 2–3).

In those two verses, the words *bless/blessed/blessing* appear five times. The pastor who gave the sermon explained that a core meaning of the original Hebrew word for "blessing" was the sense of being present. God was promising to be present with Abraham; his very presence was a sign of his favor and provision in Abraham's life.

While listening to the sermon, I realized I had not been present with the widows and children of India. My well-intentioned compassion fell short of what God expected from me. The sense of calling was almost overwhelming. I needed to go to India.

So a few months later, I boarded a plane bound for central India, where I spent ten days meeting with groups of widows, praying with them, and offering what comfort I could. My hosts took me to the city of Yavatmal in the state of Maharashtra and there invited me to stand on a platform and speak from my heart.

"My mother was a widow like you," I said. "I was nine years old when I lost my father. From then on, our house was filled with fear and despair . . ."

As I spoke, what had been a financial commitment became a personal connection. My story was no longer only about me; it was also about these precious families and how God would use me and my story to bless their lives.

I can't express on paper how powerful that experience was for me. I knew this was why God had drawn my attention to that original television report. He wasn't just calling me to write a check or provide material support to a good cause. He was calling me to be present with others, to share my story and my pain with them. He was changing my orbit.

As I held the hands of the Indian widows and prayed with them, I felt connected by our shared experience, our shared pain. Though we came from different cultures, my story intersected with theirs. And through the bonds we made, God began to transform my pain into healing power and blessing.

Those days with the widows and orphans cemented for me what I'd first seen in my experiences with the fatherless boys much closer to home.

What about you? Who are the people God is bringing into your life? What burdens do they carry and how has God uniquely positioned you to help them with those burdens?

We cannot predict the people God will bring into our orbits or when we'll be uniquely capable of meeting their needs. All we can do is commit ourselves to paying attention, being open, and orbiting those he calls us to serve. He gives us what we need. He offers us the abundance that comes only through his miraculous provision.

Serving in this capacity can be a frightening step of faith, especially when we're already feeling stretched and tested, when wounds are still raw and hurting, or when we're sure we don't have enough. But when we approach our lives with faith that what we give will be returned to us in ways we cannot even imagine, God steps in to show the way.

God's Rhythm of Provision for You: Orbiting

Think about the scientific article that states you and I are hardwired for generosity. In John 13:35, Jesus tells his disciples they will be known for their love. Our individual and collective selfishness reflects our sin and brokenness.

Our journey to this point has involved faith to believe in God's capacity, faith to invite him into areas of our lives, and faith to persevere through challenges as he reorders our lives. God always responds to our faith with guidance and provision.

Ask God to open doors for you to serve in a community. Ask him to fill you with his joy as you serve in love. This is the antidote for selfishness.

In the area of orbiting, evaluate yourself on a scale of 1 to 10:

1 To this point, I have seen no connection between serving in love and my fulfillment or God's blessing.

5 I am just beginning this journey of putting others first.

I understand that miracles of provision often happen in community.

10 I see the connection and seek to honor others and God through my service.

Your score: _____

Enter your score on page 211.

8

One to Another

The Heart of Community

Imagine there is a lock over the place in your heart that holds your sense of purpose and fulfillment. You must open the lock to uncover the fullness of what God wants you to experience in life.

Fortunately, God has also given you a key. Yet there's a trick: your key doesn't fit your lock. No one's key fits their own lock. Because God has designed us to live together in community, he has given us keys that only fit the locks of other people. Your heart can be unlocked only by someone else as you serve them, love them, encourage them, pray for them, and live generously toward them.

This is what community, fully realized, looks like.

This fourth and final aspect of Jesus's miracle of provision is much deeper, and much richer, than most of us realize.

In fact, it wasn't until that life-changing trip to India that I understood the true miracle of God's provision. His promise to fill my life with abundance depended on not only my relationship with him but also my relationships with the people he put in my orbit.

This is a concept the Reimagine Group calls "One to Another." More than ninety times the Bible reminds us of the importance of our connections to "one another." We are admonished to bear one another's burdens, humble ourselves to one another, honor one another, serve one another, be devoted to one another, pray for one another, and, of course, love one another.

Over and over, we're called to live generously in community with one another. This isn't a suggestion or a nice idea. It's the simplest description of what God wants from us. Yet we seem to fight it every way we can. We pay lip service to loving one another even as we demand control over our own actions, possessions, and schedules. In *Life Together*, Dietrich Bonhoeffer writes, "The person who loves their dream of community will destroy community, but the person who loves those around them will create community."[1]

In Galatians 5:14, Paul writes, "For the entire law is fulfilled in keeping this one command: 'Love your neighbor as yourself.'" It may seem, at first, as if Paul forgot the other great commandment Jesus gave—to love God with our whole hearts, souls, and minds. But there are no mistakes in the Bible, and on reflection, the better conclusion is that Paul knows our love for God is played out through our generosity toward others.

This is central to our relationship with God.

Living Generously

As we've already seen, most people equate generous living exclusively with open wallets. They embrace what we call transactional generosity. This is what happens when someone gives something tangible, like money or products or even time, with no expectation of relationship. For years, I engaged with the program for widows in India this way. My financial gifts supported the Christian pastors and community organizers on the ground and allowed them to buy necessary tools to help physically provide for and protect the widows and their children.

This kind of giving is important. Some needs are so big that it takes the resources of many people to begin to meet them. When we make a donation to relief efforts after a war or famine or earthquake has devastated some far-flung corner of the world, our transactional generosity—and the generosity of millions of others—provides support for the few people who have the expertise to be valuable on the ground. However, transactional generosity is only a starting point. It's not what brings us to the place of spiritual and emotional abundance. It's not yet living one to another.

Relationships mattered more to Jesus than resources. In Matthew 23:23, he calls out the rigid, tradition-bound temple leaders: "Woe to you, teachers of the law and Pharisees, you hypocrites! You give a tenth of your spices—mint, dill and cumin. But you have neglected the more important matters of the law—justice, mercy and faithfulness. You should have practiced the latter, without neglecting the former."

We too are called to practice relational generosity, which is where living one to another happens. These kinds of engagements are deeply personal. Relational generosity is about more than giving away money and various material goods. Instead, it is about inviting vulnerable people into our lives. It's what Steve, the pastor I mentioned in chapter 2, did when he invited a troubled teen to live with his family. It's what I did when I packed my bags and flew halfway around the world to meet the widows in India face-to-face and share their emotional and physical burdens.

Living one to another means making friends with people who need friends, giving time to people who need time, giving forgiveness to people who need to be forgiven, and giving love to those who feel unlovable.

One clear example I've seen of the difference between transactional and relational generosity happened years ago when a company I worked with gathered a group of employees to volunteer for a day of service in the inner city. I arrived half an hour late to find the team scattered around a house, tackling some much-needed landscaping projects. They were working hard, and with good intentions, but something seemed off.

As I was chatting with the volunteer coordinator, we noticed suspicious faces staring out through the windows of the house. They don't look happy to see us, I thought. I asked the volunteer coordinator if anyone had gone to the house to introduce themselves. After checking with the others, he realized they hadn't.

No wonder the people in the house were glaring at us! They must have wondered what all these people were doing in their yard. We immediately pulled together a few of the volunteers and knocked on the front door. The coordinator explained what we were doing and who had asked us to come, and then we invited some of the kids down to the park to play basketball.

Trimming the shrubs outside the house was transactional, but engaging with the people inside the house was relational.

Whom Do We Serve?

The parable of the Good Samaritan is one of the best-known stories in the Bible. You probably already know the basics of the famous parable: a man, who happens to be Jewish, is walking on a road when he is mugged. The thieves take everything, even his clothes, and leave him half dead in a ditch.

Two men, each one a respected member of his Jewish community, walk by the man without stopping. Jesus doesn't explain why they don't stop. Perhaps they were busy. Perhaps they thought they didn't have the skills to make a difference. Perhaps they were afraid for their own safety. Their reasons for not responding don't matter; Jesus shows us only their lack of response.

Then a Samaritan comes along, sees the injured man, and helps him.

In first-century Israel, Samaritans were a racial and religious minority distrusted by everyone—Romans and Jews alike. In fact, strict fundamentalist Jews were so suspicious of being "contaminated" by impure Samaritans that they would travel days out of their way to avoid walking through a Samaritan neighborhood. And the feeling was, by some accounts, mutual. The Samaritans believed their worship and traditions were holier than those of traditional Jews and that their persecution was a sign God honored them most. They too looked down on others.

It's not a stretch to look to today's culture and find parallels, even in the church, of people who are not respected or who are judged.

In Jesus's story, though, the Samaritan did not hold a grudge or pass by the bloody and broken man in the ditch. Instead, perhaps at great risk to himself, he helped the injured man. The Samaritan's generosity was not expressed from a safe distance—by tossing the injured man canned goods and a religious tract from the opposite side of the road. No, the Samaritan got his hands dirty. He bandaged the injured stranger, cleaned him up, put him on a donkey, and brought him to an inn, where he paid for the man's care. His actions were personal, messy, and costly.

Jesus's message in telling this story is clear: Whom does God call us to serve? Who is our neighbor? It is the person in front of us, regardless of what they look like, what they believe, or where they live. Our neighbor is the driver in traffic who honks at us, the surly clerk at the department store, the smug people next door who look as if they have the perfect life, the homeless person asking for money on the sidewalk, the immigrant man who walks the track at the gym every morning, the guy at the office who wants to argue politics, the elderly woman in the back pew at church who is seemingly friendless, and even our rebellious teenager who doesn't want to listen to a word we say. Our neighbor is anybody and everybody who crosses our paths, anyone we happen to notice, anyone with a need or hurt, anyone who opposes us or offends us, anyone who intersects with our lives in even the smallest, most insignificant way.

Caring for our neighbors is truly living one to another.

I began thinking about all of this a few years ago after I read an article in the newspaper about how residents of a well-to-do suburban neighborhood were upset about a request for them to give holiday gifts and bonuses to the sanitation workers in their community. The story made me stop and consider, for the first time, the people who come once a week to collect my trash.

It was cold, but one day I waited outside for them as they made their rounds. When the giant, smelly, noisy truck pulled up in front of my house, I stepped up and looked each worker in the eye as I thanked them, gave them a Christmas gift, and told them how much I appreciated that they got out of bed and worked on such a miserable day.

Afterward, I wondered, *Who else am I missing?* Asking this drove me to sit down and make a list of the people in my daily life I was not praying for. The list was uncomfortably long—the person who cut my hair, the person who did my taxes, the person who boarded my dog, and the person who washed my car. I was surrounded by a community I barely noticed.

Scripture repeatedly encourages us to look at abundance as the fruit we produce, not the assets we possess. God's promise is that he will fill our lives not with material goods but with people—often people we have the opportunity to bless. When we pass the bread and fish on to those who are near us, God promises to refill our empty hands and bless us even more. And more often than not, he uses the people around us to bring that provision.

Jesus once told a group of prominent Pharisees:

When you give a luncheon or dinner, do not invite your friends, your brothers or sisters, your relatives, or your rich neighbors; if you do, they may invite you back and so you will be repaid. But when you give a banquet, invite the poor, the crippled, the lame, the blind, and you will be blessed. Although they cannot repay you, you will be repaid at the resurrection of the righteous. (Luke 14:12–14)

My company, the Reimagine Group, produced a short film called *Banquet* based on this interaction between Jesus and the Pharisees. In this film, the poor who had been invited to the banquet had no name cards to designate where they should sit. However, the more well-to-do invitees did have name cards. Our main character proceeded to tear up the name cards, symbolizing that all were welcome at the banquet.

The fact is that all of us have been invited to a banquet we have no right to attend and offered an indescribable gift we have no merit to receive. Furthermore, this advice from Jesus should shape whom we invite to our own meals and change how and to whom we offer our own gifts.

The Sharing Economy

The largest hotelier in the world (Airbnb) owns no rooms, the largest taxi provider (Uber) owns no vehicles, and the largest media company (Facebook) produces no original content. Instead, they've harnessed billions of dollars of unexpected value from existing but underutilized assets of private housing, transportation, and pockets of time that individuals are offering, short term, to others who want them. As people have pushed past the traditional barriers between business and personal spaces, unexpected value has been unlocked and unleashed.

So much here reflects the ideas of one to another living. People are welcoming one another into their homes, into their cars, into their personal stories, providing huge opportunities to connect with neighbors and others.

But like other things we've looked at, these examples are more complicated. When we push past the shiny photos of smiling people and the glowing testimonials, the modern sharing economy is still transaction based. Those people providing services make money (or, in the case of a free social media app such as Facebook, are given a free channel to share their content). That's not true sharing—it's just the latest way for businesses to turn a profit.

If we want to see an example of what a true sharing economy looks like, we need to go back to the communities built by the first Christians.

Not long after Jesus's death and resurrection, something amazing happened: people who barely knew each other began to share with one another.

Peter preached a powerful message to a diverse audience of people who were visiting Jerusalem. Three thousand people were baptized and joined the church that day (Acts 2). Those early Christians came together from various countries and spoke many languages. I imagine they also had some different cultural traditions, foods, and lifestyles. The early church was composed of both wealthy landowners and people with needs. Yet Acts 2:44 tells us, "All the believers were together and had everything in common." And Acts 4:32 says, "All the believers were one in heart and mind. No one claimed that any of their possessions was their own, but they shared everything they had."

The church's love for Jesus, whose sacrificial generosity of offering his own life was the greatest possible example of sharing, overshadowed their differences and filled them with love for one another. Full of God's grace and love, they gave away whatever they had—possessions, acts of service, and acts of compassion—without any discussion of repayment.

"At the present time your plenty will supply what they need, so that in turn their plenty will supply what you need. The goal is equality," writes Paul in his second letter to the Corinthians (8:14).

The believers of the newborn church described in the book of Acts saw everything they had as belonging to God, and every person around them as a neighbor, regardless of where they were born.

So what changed?

We forgot that "we are," as my friend Pastor Darryl Ford says, "not just saved from something but also saved to something. And that something is a life of service and community."

When the disciples, and then the crowd, took the bread and fish and passed them on, they acknowledged that what was happening was not just about them. This was not their platform, nor was Jesus offering them a bigger blessing or gift than he gave anyone else. This was a chance for the entire community, collectively, to reflect back the light of God's goodness to one another.

Jesus said to love our neighbors as ourselves. And because it's easier to love a neighbor who looks like us, we start isolating ourselves.

Darryl preached a sermon recently about the different ways most people experience community today, and the first two look uncomfortably familiar. First are the "soup communities." These are the places where everyone is so similar—in race, age, income, and lifestyle—that they're almost interchangeable. These communities are monocultural and safe.[2]

190

But as we've seen, Jesus never called us to be safe.

Second are the "salad communities." Diversity, like what the early Christians experienced after Pentecost, is publicly celebrated. But privately, those in the salad communities still want things to be comfortable. They cover over the elements they don't like with some sort of "salad dressing." The celebration of the community happens in name only, and the majority culture covers over anything that is difficult to deal with.

There is a third community, what Darryl calls "pressure cooker communities." Pressure cookers, according to Darryl, are good for making stews. The heat and pressure make each flavor "bleed"—or blend—into one another. A pepper in a stew pot, for example, doesn't stay isolated; it influences the experience and flavor of everything else in the pot. This blending of flavors in a church setting makes for the type of radical love in which people take prayerful and thoughtful risks in relationships.

Darryl's words challenged me. For years, I had thought the Bible was calling *me* to help those in need. I held myself above others. But in a pressure cooker environment, we can't hold back or stand apart. Community isn't about *me* and *them*. In God's eyes, there is no *me* or *them*. I am not some unique flavor in God's kingdom. By serving others, I become one with them.

I went back to Scripture and discovered something I had never before noticed. Four times in the book of Psalms, David says, "I am poor and needy" (40:17; 70:5; 86:1; 109:22). That set me on my heels. If the king of Israel saw himself that way, why did I think I was somehow better?

First John 3:16 says, "This is how we know what love is: Jesus Christ laid down his life for us. And we ought to lay down our lives for our brothers and sisters."

191

God calls us to a radical life of service. This is true community and true one to another living.

Barriers to Love, Provision, and True Community

Seems simple, right? But clearly it's not.

We've seen that God hardwired the human brain for generosity, and then he showed us over and over again in Scripture how important it is. Why, then, is this idea of one to another living so hard for us to live out? Is our selfishness so great? Sadly, yes.

The attitude of scarcity, fear, and isolation that is drowning so many people today—including so many Christ-followers—is the direct result of a spiritual battle against God's promise of provision. The battle is fiercest in the ways we view the people around us. This is because Satan knows this is where some of our greatest weaknesses lie.

In 2007, researchers at the University of California–San Diego published the findings of a study referred to as "The Sharing Game." In it, the interviewer offered each participant two options:

1. They could receive $7, in which case an unknown person would receive $9.
2. They could receive $5, in which case an unknown person would receive $3.

The overwhelming majority of participants chose option number two, in which an unknown person would not receive more than they did, even though that meant the participants received less than they would have otherwise. I was shocked to read this. People simply did not want an unknown neighbor to get more—and they would even accept less for themselves to ensure this outcome.[3]

When we're caught in Satan's lie of radical individualism, believing we can rely only on ourselves, we fail and are left with a deep sense of fear and despair. Satan throws whatever he can at us to pull us apart, to make us see one another— God's creations—as somehow less worthy, less deserving of our time and attention. He does this because when we are fractured, we are easier to control. When we are frightened, we are open to his lies.

Jesus told us to "love your neighbor as yourself" (Matthew 22:39), but Satan convinces us that this clear instruction is open to interpretation. "After all," he tells us, "who is your neighbor, really? What about the person who doesn't look like you or believe what you believe or live the way you want to live? Can you really trust them?"

Many of us were raised with the motto "God helps those who help themselves." Satan has used this cliché—which isn't found in the Bible—to tempt even the most devout Christians to justify their isolation, reticence, and deep feelings of scarcity. He has assured them that they should clutch the blessings they've been given, keeping the bread and fish instead of passing them along—not because they're selfish or unkind but because they're worried about how they will feed their families tomorrow.

When we have a scarcity mind-set, we hold on to what we have been given instead of freely giving it to others—and God's miracle of provision stops.

"Help yourself first" is not God's message. Instead, he tells us to "cast all [our] anxiety on him because he cares for [us]" (1 Peter 5:7).

One extremely painful thing that has come out of our fast-tracked electronic society is that the people around us stop being individuals and start blending together into one interchangeable, impersonal collection. We communicate, and sometimes even worship, via a screen and a keyboard rather than face-to-face. Instead of a community of individuals we can serve, the "others" in our lives may be only anonymous names on a computer screen, and our only interaction is wondering why their lives look so much better than ours.

Now I'm not saying electronic communication is a bad thing. I'm as attached to my email and cell phone as anyone else. But I do think we need to be wary of letting it lull us into opting out of connections with other living, breathing people.

I believe Satan cares less about a group of people getting together on Sunday morning to sing songs and recite words than he does a single individual who goes out into the world and starts changing lives.

The Risk of Vulnerability

A few years ago, our company, the Reimagine Group, helped organize a five-week program of "loving generously" events for sixty-two churches. The core message of the materials for the program was one to another, encouraging each person to minister to the vulnerable and to reconcile with anyone they needed to. Meetings were organized all over Atlanta, culminating on Pentecost Sunday. I had the chance to speak to groups of pastors from throughout the city about their goals for the coming five weeks.

Using Luke 14:12–14, the passage about inviting those who cannot repay you to a banquet, as my foundation, I asked the pastors to challenge each of their congregants to invite one vulnerable person into their lives in the coming forty days or to seek out one person they needed to reconcile with.

The program went off without a hitch. There were multichurch celebrations across the city, and we heard dozens of stories about how communities were touched as thousands of Christians served and volunteered together. However, I couldn't shake the sense that it all felt programmatic and decidedly nonrelational. Where was the reconciliation? Where was the personal connection? When invited to love generously, most people responded by bringing food to a shelter, volunteering at a school, or doing a service project with their friends.

They were living "soup community" lives, holding themselves back and doing what felt safe, when what I'd hoped for was a messy stew of personalities and needs blending together into a true community. They gave of their excess when what God calls us to do is give of our essence.

Did something hold them back from taking that next step?

Is something holding you back?

As I've talked to people since then, I've found that people have a deep aversion to the vulnerability that comes from truly engaging in community. Learning to see ourselves as part of an interconnected, holy, unguarded creation can be disconcerting for those of us who were raised with a strong dose of New England stoicism.

Medically, it has been proven that loneliness is harmful to our health. Heart disease, dementia, and premature death have all been linked to loneliness. We were built for community.[4]

Yet vulnerability is hard for some of us to talk about, let alone try. Sharing our deepest needs and most intimate concerns with others gives them power in our lives. I've certainly had my seasons of holding back. *What if I share my heart and no one responds?*

Vulnerability is part of God's perfect plan. It is how he brings us to a place of deep dependence on him—and in closely aligned orbit with one another.

A few months ago, Lisa and I were visiting with a small group of friends. We'd been meeting together for seven years, but this night was special, because one of the couples spoke up and said, "We need to tell you something we haven't said to anyone before." They went on to share some difficult things that had been happening in their family for some time and how afraid they were.

The mood in the room shifted as their risky honesty washed over us. We gathered around our friends, laid our hands on them, and began to pray harder than we ever had before. Then we began to talk and to really share. The entire group has operated on a different, more trusting level since then because these dear friends were willing to share so openly and to invite us to live one to another.

If we believe God uses community to provide for us, and we are going to rely on the provision he promises, then we must learn to trust the neighbors God puts in our lives. We can live one to another, or we can try to do it all ourselves.

Living one to another isn't easy. Learning to abide in community (and vulnerability) can be a difficult and sometimes painful journey. And Satan fights us *every* step of the way.

We cannot succeed in our own strength. Thankfully, we don't have to! God promises repeatedly to honor our service to others and to show us the way. Our model is Jesus, who, motivated by love, left his home to join a broken creation. We can love because he first loved us. We can sacrifice because he first sacrificed for us. We can take risks because he risked himself for us. His love and Spirit compel us to die to ourselves—just as he died.

When we are open to God, he will provide.

One of the people I work with, Patty, had a car break down a few years ago, not long after her family moved to the Atlanta area. It was too expensive to fix, so Patty and her husband set out to buy a replacement car.

At the time, she and I were starting to work through the content for this book, specifically the topic of casting oneself on community in times of need. Leery of buying a used car from an unknown dealership, she decided to put feet to these principles. She sent a text to the short list of everyone she knew in the area, asking if anyone had a used car to sell or could recommend a place to buy a car. A few people texted suggestions. But one woman replied, "Give me a call when you have a moment."

Patty called, and the woman said, "It's the oddest thing. My husband and I have been talking about replacing our Toyota 4Runner, but we both felt the Lord prompting us not to sell it. He wanted us to give it away, which we were open to, but we didn't know anyone who needed a car. So last night we prayed, 'All right, Lord, we know you want us to give the car away. Please show us the person you want us to give it to.' I woke up this morning, and there was your text." They gave their car to Patty's family.

I love this story because it beautifully illustrates how vulnerability, in the context of community, provides the opportunity for God to move through the capacity of people to meet one another's needs. The opportunity to cast ourselves on our communities is deep and rich. It draws us to a level of faith we could never find on our own and opens us to blessings we can't even imagine.

Well Done

Years ago, Lisa and I were involved with an organization that rescues some of the millions of people trapped in bonded slavery. During this time, I had a dream. I was standing before Jesus at the judgment. I saw a young man I didn't recognize, although I somehow knew he was an evangelist. The Lord said to me, "Well done."

I felt confused until I saw, in that mysterious way that happens only in dreams, that this was the son of a woman who had been rescued from trafficking through the ministry we served.

We don't always see the full effect of how we choose to live or the long-term impact of a simple choice to invest in a person. The three servants in the parable of the bags of gold certainly didn't. But each gift we invest in a person when we prayerfully, thoughtfully, and intentionally minister to those in need creates a ripple effect, which spreads across God's kingdom.

Your willingness to have lunch with and listen to a young person just starting their career, or to make a few phone calls of introduction on their behalf, might change the trajectory of their life. Or your choice to bring dinner to a mom struggling with preschoolers while her husband travels for business, and then to stay and share her evening, might open a window of spiritual or emotional growth that changes her life.

For years, Lisa and I have offered a spare bedroom in our home to anyone who needed it. One woman lived with us for three years while she was establishing a crisis pregnancy counseling center in our area. After she moved away, she told us that during the time she lived with us, more than one thousand women chose to have their babies. Through a simple act of offering what we had, we became a small part of that miracle of God's provision.

Are you willing to be vulnerable, to lean into your pain and persevere through your wilderness experiences? Are you willing to boldly enter the wildernesses of others? Who is your fatherless child, your Indian widow?

Imagine if each of us reconciled with one person and invited one vulnerable person into our lives per year. Imagine what God could do with that kind of abundance.

As each year passes in my journey through life, I learn a little more about the ways God uses us, and I gain new appreciation for the complex dance he choreographs. He shows us capacity beyond what we could possibly imagine, blessing what we offer him as he brings each of us in and out of the wilderness. But it is here, in the communities of people he has put around us, that we will find our way past the immediate fears and crushing weight of doubt. It is through the sometimes painful, slow process of letting go of ourselves and learning to orbit the Creator in service to the people he created that we find the physical, emotional, and spiritual provision that will carry us through our time on earth.

When Jesus said, "I have come that they may have life, and have it to the full" (John 10:10), he promised us an abundant life, not an abundant lifestyle. We are not promised material blessings but instead deeper, more meaningful blessings that God wants to produce in us. In other words, the abundant life has to do with the fruitfulness of our lives.

Someday, when we stand before God, he will show us the impact our gifts have made. And we, like the men and women in Matthew 25, will say, "Lord, I don't remember doing any of this. I don't remember having any huge impact."

I am convinced he will answer, "Whatever you did for one of the least of these brothers and sisters of mine, you did for me" (Matthew 25:40).

The life of abundance God promises is yours. The bread and fish are lying before you. Will you take them and share them with the people around you, trusting there will be enough? Will you continue the miracle of provision God offers?

God's Rhythm of Provision for You: Living One to Another

Read Matthew 25:35–36 and write down the six categories of people Jesus identifies with (the hungry, the sick, etc.). Part of reflecting God's love is having eyes to see the unseen in society. Think of some vulnerable people in your neighborhood or workplace you can reach out to. Consider asking these people to tell you more about their stories. You can share in the provision God has given you by serving those around you. Instead of looking for ways to help via transactional generosity, live one to another by looking for ways to serve using relational generosity.

Ultimately, your life can be a blessing to Jesus when you serve the least. He loved us first when we were his enemies. Let this empower you to live to be a blessing.

In the area of living one to another, evaluate yourself on a scale of 1 to 10:

1 I am pretty isolated and not in community.

5 I am in community but have not gotten a lot out of it. I am willing to take steps to serve others.

10 I am committed to community. I see that as I serve, God may use me but also meet my needs.

1   2   3   4   5   6   7   8   9   10

Your score: _____

Enter your score on page 211.

Conclusion

The Secret of Enough

I wrote this book because of the disconnect between God being "the God of more" and such a large majority of people, even the rich, having a scarcity mind-set rooted in fear. There is a true collision between the two mind-sets. Throughout this book, we have investigated God's four-step pattern of provision. However, the secret behind this pattern is God himself.

In 2011, I produced a message and video called *Reveal* based on Proverbs 25:2 (NKJV): "It is the glory of God to conceal a matter, but the glory of kings is to search out a matter." I found it ironic that the King of Glory would *get* glory from concealing things from us. The video shows the story of a father who would leave his two daughters clues for gifts and little love notes around the house when he left home. The girls would excitedly run around finding these treasures, showing them to their mother. It struck me that God desires for us to seek him out, to pursue an intimate relationship with him, just as those little girls would seek out the gifts from their father. After all, he is our Heavenly Father and our Provider. My pastor defines glory as "satisfaction"; God gets glory as he conceals things. He promises us satisfaction as we discover his clues, guidance, and gifts.

Think of the promises he gives us through Scripture. In Hebrews 11:6, God declares that he "is a rewarder of those who diligently seek him" (NKJV). Second Chronicles 16:9 says, "The eyes of the Lord range throughout the earth to strengthen those whose hearts are fully committed to him" (NIV). This rhythm of seeking and drawing near speaks to the same rhythm of provision that we have discussed throughout this book. God continually shows us his desire to draw close to us and that we would draw close to him. Behind all of this is his desire to have an intimate relationship with us. He is seeking seekers! Seekers will find him, his rewards, and his provision. We can understand this because, oftentimes, in intimate human relationships, the love of another is proven, so to speak, when we take the time to draw out the other's deep feelings, cares, concerns, or desires.

Wherever you were when you started reading, I hope you found yourself in the story of Jesus's physical provision on the hillside.

Are you like the boy in the Gospel story who supplied the fish and bread? Are you holding on to some small gift, uncertain how God can use it . . . or you? Do your meager resources leave you uncertain about helping yourself, let alone another person? "Really?" you ask God. "You want this? But it's just a fish!"

God may be a bit of a stranger to you. You may be checking him out for the first time and committing feels like a big step. You may have enough emotional and physical provision for today, but you have lingering questions about tomorrow. It may feel like a challenge to hand over what you have to the God who already has plenty and then trust that he, in turn, will give your gift back in abundance. Maybe you should just share a piece of your bread first and see what happens?

It's difficult to pass the basket of food to someone else and trust there will be enough for you. But that's exactly what God promises will happen. "Fear not," he says over and over. The God of abundance has the capacity to provide.

Or perhaps you are more like the disciples. You've been following Jesus for a long time, and you're committed to him—at least it appears that way. You go to church and even tithe. But you're confused. At times, you see God's provision in your life, sometimes in amazing ways, but then you find yourself facing the same recurring struggles and doubts. The mortgage is due, both the church and the PTA are asking for volunteers, your kids are asking why they need to practice "shooter drills" in school, and Facebook is full of videos of starving refugee families. Soon you find yourself wrestling with the same things you just worked through.

You so badly want to believe Jesus is real, that he can and will provide for you. Yet you teeter-totter on this scale of belief, recognizing God's hand in your life and then wondering in a panic if he is going to show up again.

Are there places in your spiritual practice that have become so routine, so familiar, that you've lost sight of the true miracle of it all? Is God calling you to dig deeper? What corners of your life haven't you opened up to him yet?

This is where I still find myself sometimes, after years of study and hundreds of opportunities to see God's miraculous intervention in my own life. This relationship dance with the Savior takes a lifetime to master.

As long as we're human, and prone to misunderstandings and temptation, we will feel doubt at times. The wilderness can seem overwhelming. We will be fearful. But God is always present, calling us, offering a miraculous meal of abundance.

These days when I look at the story of the miracle on the hillside, I'm drawn specifically to the experience of the disciple John. His Gospel account is more detailed than the other three. I wonder if that is because he had a more personal response to this event. We know he was a fisherman before he started to follow Jesus. It's interesting, then, that his Gospel is the only one that specifically mentions that after Jesus broke the bread, he did the same with the fish. John knew exactly what a fish weighed and how many people a single fish could feed. He'd spent years trying to fill empty nets with enough food to feed his community. And now this Teacher, on dry land, had filled baskets with fish from practically nothing.

God took the thing John knew best and did something radically and miraculously different with it. I wonder if this is the day John's relationship with Jesus changed to something deeper, something more committed. In his Gospel, John refers to himself as "the one Jesus loved" (John 20:2), and in the years after Jesus's death, he was a passionate Christ-follower, penning four more books that guide Christians today.

Wherever you are, and whatever you believed when you started reading this book, please know God has a plan for you. He knows your future—and it is not driven by scarcity or fear. Instead, it's a life filled with holiness, presence, and purpose.

You too have a place in the story God is writing.

Cross-Shaped Generosity

As I look at what God has done in my life over the past number of years, I can truly report I have never been happier, more fulfilled, or more certain of God's deep commitment to providing for me as I live in full relationship with him. He has taken the pain and dysfunction of my past and replaced them with the blessing of his abundance. He has rescued me from the dark, isolated world where I thought I was alone.

I don't always understand why God is calling us to certain opportunities and away from others, but we need to follow him in hard places of service and sacrifice. In "The Liturgy of Abundance," Walter Brueggemann speaks of this kind of sacrificial, relational generosity as "cruciform" or cross-shaped generosity. It reflects the full abundance of what Christ offers us. His idea that generosity starts with a vertical connection between a person and God and then is completed by a horizontal generosity that connects people to one another is consistent with what we've explored together in this book.[1]

First, we've seen that God has created *capacity* in us, in others, and in his creation. The faith to see capacity changes us, and God promises he will reward those who believe in him and diligently seek him.

Second, we've seen that inviting God and his holiness into the specific details of our lives makes a crucial difference.

When we do so, a transformation process begins. God promises to do amazing things when we *consecrate* who we are and what we have for his purposes and glory.

Persevering in *challenges* becomes a furnace that converts our "silica" to "silicon." We change in the hand of God and, by his method, are humbled. He promises never to leave us or forsake us in this process. Like Daniel, we can catch a glimpse of the One in the furnace with us who "looks like a son of the gods" (Daniel 3:25).

Throughout this process, our souls are marinated and softened so we can be useful and effective in *community*, this communal or horizontal expression of the cross. In humility, we serve others; our vulnerability and honesty create a "stew" in which our lives blend together with those of others.

Discovering the willingness to let go of our own orbits and instead sacrifice everything to the communities around us is the secret and foundation to experiencing the "enough" that God promises.

God's provision has nothing to do with how much money we have or how other people treat us or how much power we have in the marketplace. It's entirely about the relationships—first with God himself and then with the people he brings into our lives so we can serve them.

If you're struggling with a feeling of loss but are not sure how to start living in this new, freeing way, ask yourself this: How can Jesus uniquely love the world through me? You are a person like no other. You bring your own story, your own experiences, and your own unique opportunities to share. And through those experiences, you will find an abundant well of peace.

As we invite God into our capacity, consecrate our lives to him, succumb to being broken, and seek community, he will enter our lives in fresh ways to reorder and provide.

A Lifetime Journey

None of us will get this right all the time. I have fallen again and again over the years, sometimes so low I couldn't even pray. And time after time, God has rescued me from my doubt and weakness. He has shown me he can be trusted, even when I cannot see the way out. God has been faithful to me in every way, and at the end of the day, I feel like Peter when he said in John 6:68, "Lord, to whom shall we go? You have the words of eternal life."

God is faithful. He sees your intentions and hears your heart. His grace and mercy can fill in the gaps of your broken life and satisfy all the places where you think there is not enough. If you are in a place of fear and doubt, or if you're holding on to something precious that God is calling you to commit—your time, your resources, your vulnerability, your gifts, your family—think of the little boy on the hillside. Or the little boy Jaden, who lost his parents but chose to give joy to others through his smile. Trust God, knowing that if he was able to do miracles in their lives, then he can also do something amazing in yours.

"I have told you these things, so that in me you may have peace," Jesus said. "In this world you will have trouble. But take heart! I have overcome the world" (John 16:33).

It's time to free yourself from the dangerous cycle of fear. If you are living in a place of "not enough," either financially or emotionally, remember that these four aspects of

God's provision—capacity, consecration, challenges, and community—are the same ones Jesus used to turn a simple meal into enough to feed thousands, and they are integral to understanding your relationship with God.

He has unequivocally promised to provide for us—if we follow him. In the life he crafts for you, God guarantees you will have enough.

Your Scores

Congratulations on taking the bold step of self-assessment. I recognize it's impossible for a number to capture all the details of a person's lived experience, but my hope is that these scores give you a *relative* sense of how you are doing in each area and which areas may deserve more of your attention than others.

Chapter 1: _____   Chapter 5: _____

Chapter 2: _____   Chapter 6: _____

Chapter 3: _____   Chapter 7: _____

Chapter 4: _____   Chapter 8: _____

Total: _____

Post this total score at www.thegodguarantee.com/score, and we will give you access to a nationally recognized short film to encourage you.

Notes

Introduction

1. Steve Hartman, "After Losing Parents, 6-Year-Old Embarks on Smile Mission," *CBS News*, August 7, 2015, http://www.cbsnews.com/news /after-losing-parents-6-year-old-embarks-on-mission/.

2. Brené Brown, *Daring Greatly: How the Courage to Be Vulnerable Transforms the Way We Live, Love, Parent, and Lead* (London: Penguin Books, 2012), 9.

3. "The Impact of Wealth and Success, How Much Is Enough?" *UBS United States*, April 28, 2015, https://www.ubs.com/us/en/wealth/news /wealth-management-americas-news.html/en/2015/04/28/ubs-investor -watch-2015-2Q.html.

4. Walter Brueggemann, "The Liturgy of Abundance, the Myth of Scarcity," *The Christian Century*, March 24, 1999, https://www.christian century.org/article/2012-01/liturgy-abundance-myth-scarcity.

5. "5 Reasons Millennials Stay Connected to Church," *Barna Group, Millennials and Generations*, September 17, 2013, https://www.barna .com/research/5-reasons-millennials-stay-connected-to-church/.

6. "Hubble Reveals Observable Universe Contains Ten Times More Galaxies than Previously Thought," NASA, October 13, 2016, www.nasa .gov/feature/goddard/2016/hubble-reveals-observable-universe-contains -10-times-more-galaxies-than-previously-thought; Marina Koren, "The Universe Just Got 10 Times More Interesting," *Atlantic*, October 14, 2016, www.theatlantic.com/science/archive/2016/10/so-many-galaxies/504185/.

213

7. Brueggemann, "The Liturgy of Abundance."

8. *Dictionary.com*, s.v. "consecrate," accessed April 3, 2017, www.diction ary.com/browse/consecrate.

Chapter 1 The Land of What Could Be

1. David Dellinger, *From Yale to Jail: The Life Story of a Moral Dissenter* (Eugene, OR: Wipf and Stock Publishers, 1993), 418.

2. "A Telecom Story with Dr. Steven Shepherd," University of Southern California Marshall School of Business, accessed February 21, 2017, http://www.marshall.usc.edu/videos/telecom-story-dr-steven-shepard.

3. "Willow Bark," University of Maryland Medical Center, accessed April 3, 2017, www.umm.edu/health/medical/altmed/herb/willow-bark.

4. Martin Ryan, "Sea Urchins Could Contain the Genetic Key to Curing Some Diseases," University of St. Andrews, July 6, 2012, www.st-andrews .ac.uk/news/archive/2012/title,88759,en.php.

5. "Penicillin," *Wikipedia*, accessed March 28, 2017, www.en.wikipedia .org/wiki/Penicillin.

6. Paul F Torrence, "Owed to Nature: Medicines from Tropical Forests," Rainforest Trust, January 26, 2013, www.rainforesttrust.org/news/owed-to -nature-medicines-from-tropical-forests/.

7. Mark Fidelman, "Meet the Top 30 Most Influential Photographers on the Web," *Huffington Post*, July 9, 2014, http://www.huffingtonpost .com/mark-fidelman/meet-the-top-30-most-photography_b_5566091.html.

8. Max De Pree, *Leadership Is an Art* (New York: Doubleday, 2004), 11.

9. Jim Collins, *Good to Great: Why Some Companies Make the Leap . . . and Others Don't* (New York: HarperCollins, 2001), 31.

10. Henry Scougal, *The Life of God in the Soul of Man* (Seaside, OR: Rough Draft Publishing, 2012), 38.

11. Dallas Willard, *The Great Omission: Reclaiming Jesus's Essential Teachings on Discipleship* (New York: HarperCollins, 2006), 61.

Chapter 2 A Time to Plant

1. Christopher J. L. Murray, Marie Ng, and Ali Mokdad, "The Vast Majority of American Adults Are Overweight or Obese, and Weight Is a Growing Problem among US Children," Institute for Health Metrics

and Evaluation, accessed April 3, 2017, www.healthdata.org/news-release /vast-majority-american-adults-are-overweight-or-obese-and-weight -growing-problem-among; "11 Facts about Literacy in America," DoSome thing.org, accessed April 3, 2017, www.dosomething.org/us/facts/11-facts -about-literacy-america.

2. Suzanne Goldenberg, "The Doomsday Vault: The Seeds That Could Save a Post-Apocalyptic World," *The Guardian*, May 20, 2015, https://www.theguardian.com/science/2015/may/20/the-doomsday-vault -seeds-save-post-apocalyptic-world.

3. Chip Ingram, "Reimagine Stewardship," *The Promises of God*, Application Teaching.

Chapter 3 The Invisible Hand

1. Walter Brueggemann, "Enough Is Enough," *The Other Side* 37, no. 5 (November–December 2001).

2. Brueggemann, "The Liturgy of Abundance."

3. "Holy, Holiness," *Baker's Evangelical Dictionary of Biblical Theology*, Bible Study Tools, accessed April, 2017, www.biblestudytools.com/diction aries/bakers-evangelical-dictionary/holy-holiness.html.

4. "William Barclay's Daily Study Bible, Matthew 13," StudyLight.org, accessed April 3, 2017, www.studylight.org/commentaries/dsb/matthew -13.html.

5. David Ashton and Johnny Sung, *Supporting Workplace Learning for High Performance Working* (Geneva, Switzerland: International Labour Office, 2002), accessed January 17, 2017, http://citeseerx.ist.psu.edu /viewdoc/download?doi=10.1.1.629.8732&rep=rep1&type=pdf.

6. Akshat Rathi, "What's App Bought for $19 Billion, What Do Its Em ployees Get?" *The Conversation*, February 20, 2014, http://theconversation .com/whatsapp-bought-for-19-billion-what-do-its-employees-get-23496.

7. "Secularization," *Wikipedia*, January 5, 2017, https://en.wikipedia .org/wiki/Secularization.

8. Joe Weisenthal, "Goldman Sachs Says It May Be Forced to Fundamen tally Question How Capitalism Is Working," Conduent, February 3, 2016, https://www.bloomberg.com/news/articles/2016-02-03/goldman-sachs-says -it-may-be-forced-to-fundamentally-question-how-capitalism-is-working.

Chapter 4 An Acceptable Sacrifice

1. Crawford Loritts (senior pastor, Fellowship Bible Church, Roswell, GA), in discussion with the author, August 10, 2014.

2. Timothy Keller, *Counterfeit Gods: The Empty Promises of Money, Sex, and Power and the Only Hope That Matters* (New York: Viking, 2009), 155.

Chapter 5 The Wilderness and the Marketplace

1. Dr. Bill Lawrence, *Wilderness Wanderings: Learning to Live the ZigZag Life* (North Charleston, SC: CreateSpace Independent Publishing, 2016), 4.

2. Ibid., 3.

Chapter 6 Choosing the Wilderness

1. James Estrin, "Kodak's First Digital Moment," *New York Times*, August 12, 2015, www.lens.blogs.nytimes.com/2015/08/12/kodaks-first -digital-moment/?_r=1.

2. Tony Romo, "Jordan Spieth," *Time*, April 21, 2016, http://time.com /4298236/jordan-spieth-2016-time-100/.

3. "For Ellie: Spieth Stays Grounded," *Global Golf Post*, September 9, 2013, http://www.globalgolfpost.com/now/2013/09/09/for-ellie-spieth -stays-grounded.

Chapter 7 Check Your Orbit

1. Daven Hiskey, "Velcro Was Modeled After Burrs of the Burdock Plant that Stuck to Velcro's Inventor's Pants After Hunting Trip," September 9, 2011, www.todayifoundout.com/index.php/2011/09/velcro-was-modeled -after-burrs-of-the-burdock-plant-that-stuck-to-velcros-inventors-pants -after-a-hunting-trip/; Leslie Meredith, "Color E-Readers Inspired by Butterflies," Live Science, November 23, 2009, www.livescience.com/5895 -color-readers-inspired-butterflies.html; Don DeYoung, "Polar Bear— Insulation," Discovery of Design, accessed on April 3, 2017, www.dis coveryofdesign.com/id99.html; Elizabeth Redmond, "Biomimicry: Bees Inspire the Efficiency and Communication of Web Servers," January 2008, www.sustainablog.org/2008/01/biomimicry-bees-inspire-the-efficiency -and-communication-of-web-servers/.

2. Timothy Keller, *The Reason for God: Belief in an Age of Skepticism* (New York: Penguin Group, 2008), 224–26.

3. Elizabeth Svoboda, "Hard-Wired for Giving," *Wall Street Journal*, August 31, 2013, http://www.wsj.com/articles/SB10001424127887324009304 579041231971683854.

Chapter 8 One to Another

1. Dietrich Bonhoeffer, *Life Together* (Minneapolis: Fortress, 2015), 10.

2. Darryl Ford, "New Lives Means New Community," Perimeter Church, Johns Creek, Georgia, June 5, 2016, http://www.perimeter.org /series/view/radical-love/.

3. Arthur Kennelly and Edmund Fantino, "The Sharing Game: Fairness in Resource Allocation as a Function of Incentive, Gender, and Recipient Types," *Judgment and Decision Making* 2, no. 3 (June 2007): 204–16.

4. Nicole K Valtorta, Mona Kanaan, Simon Gilbody, Sara Ronzi, and Barbara Hanratty, "Loneliness and Social Isolation As Risk Factors for Coronary Heart Disease and Stroke: Systematic Review and Meta-analysis of Longitudinal Observational Studies," *Heart*, April 18, 2016, www.heart .bmj.com/content/heartjnl/102/13/1009.full.pdf.

Conclusion

1. Brueggemann, "The Liturgy of Abundance."

Jack Alexander has built and led companies in real estate, business services, and technology. Two companies that he cofounded made the Inc. 500 list, and another, in which he is a partner, made the Inc. 5000 list. He is currently chairman and founder of a software firm called Understory as well as the Reimagine Group, a content company that makes high-quality media for the church market. A previous recipient of an Ernst & Young National Entrepreneur of the Year award, Alexander is also winner of six global awards in the corporate travel and hospitality arena. In 2005, he received the Family Honors Award as a businessman who made a positive impact on the American family. He is a regular speaker, coach, and board member for a number of businesses, nonprofits, and ministries. Jack lives in Atlanta, Georgia, with his wife, Lisa. They have three adult sons and five grandchildren.